The Essential Wisdom
of the Presidents

Essential Wisdom
of the Presidents

★ ★ ★

EDITED BY

Carol Kelly-Gangi

FALL
RIVER
PRESS

To Dad with love and gratitude.

Cover design by Scott Russo
Book design by Judy Gilats

Fall River Press
122 Fifth Avenue
New York, NY 10011

ISBN: 978-1-4351-2616-9

Printed and bound in the United States of
America

10 9 8 7 6 5 4 3 2 1

Contents

Introduction

I pray Heaven bestow the best of Blessings on this House
and all that shall hereafter inhabit it. May none but honest
and wise Men ever rule under this roof.

JOHN ADAMS, *from a letter written to Abigail immediately
after moving into the White House in November
1800. In 1934, Franklin Delano Roosevelt had the
prayer carved above the fireplace in the State Room.*

IN THESE TUMULTUOUS TIMES, with the country deeply
divided on the major issues facing our nation, the words
of the presidents are imbued with an even greater meaning as Americans struggle, once again, to define the appropriate role of government and of the executive branch.

The Essential Wisdom of the Presidents gathers 370
quotations from this extraordinary group of men
who have shaped and shepherded our nation from the
beginning. From the Founding Fathers who laid the
framework for the fledgling nation to the men who led
America from times of war, depression, and crises into

times of peace and prosperity, each chief executive is represented here. All of them, in their own way, risked—and in four tragic cases—gave their very lives for the principles they espoused.

Every president has, of course, placed his individual stamp on the presidency, and the excerpts in this book reflect the divergent views and philosophies that each man held about his role as president, the sphere of his executive power, and the priorities of his administration. In the selections that follow, Thomas Jefferson speaks passionately about the price of freedom and democracy; Abraham Lincoln offers insight into the legitimate role of government; Theodore Roosevelt extols the value of preserving our natural resources; Franklin D. Roosevelt warns against the perils of relinquishing liberty to purchase temporary safety; Lyndon B. Johnson describes the painstaking process of peace; and Bill Clinton encourages us to hold on to the American Dream. Some universal themes are reflected in the excerpts as well: undying passion for America, a fervent belief in the freedoms upon which the nation was founded, the wearying nature of politics, and the longing for the domestic pleasures of home and family.

In the largest grouping of quotations, the presidents

reveal their thoughts on the presidency itself. Harry S. Truman and Dwight D. Eisenhower reflect on the necessity for a sense of humor. James K. Polk expresses his preference to attend to as much presidential business himself as possible, while Calvin Coolidge insists on delegating duties whenever practical. Benjamin Harrison and James A. Garfield comment on the isolation and loneliness of the office, and Millard Fillmore expresses his disdain for how ex-presidents are set adrift. Theodore Roosevelt and Bill Clinton agree that perhaps no president enjoyed the office more than they did.

Still other excerpts offer a more personal glimpse into the lives of the presidents. Jimmy Carter recalls the systematic racial inequality ingrained in the America of his boyhood; Ronald Reagan, George Bush, Jimmy Carter, and Barack Obama each express the love and gratitude they feel for their wives; Abraham Lincoln and Theodore Roosevelt reveal the drudgery of attending solely to work when their beloved families were away. In a dialogue that crosses time and political boundaries, the presidents also exchange views on such subjects as the value of education, the struggle for peace and the horrors of war, the relationship of business and labor, the role of religion, and the nature of American resolve.

The Essential Wisdom of the Presidents invites readers to view our nation through the eyes of the men who have each offered—in his own way—the leadership, guidance, and inspiration that have helped to shape this great nation.

Carol Kelly-Gangi
Rumson, New Jersey, 2010

Knowledge, Learning, *and* Education

Liberty cannot be preserved without general knowledge among people.

> JOHN ADAMS, "Dissertation on the Canon and the Feudal Law," 1765

It is universally admitted that a well-instructed people alone can be permanently a free people.

> JAMES MADISON, second annual message to Congress, December 5, 1810

Knowledge is power . . . knowledge is safety . . . knowledge is happiness.

> THOMAS JEFFERSON, letter to George Ticknor, November 25, 1817

The diffusion of knowledge is the only guardian of true liberty.

> JAMES MADISON, letter to George Thompson, June 30, 1825

The pursuit of knowledge itself implies a world where men are free to follow out the logic of their own ideas. It implies a world where nations are free to solve their own problems and to realize their own ideals.

JOHN F. KENNEDY, address at University of California at Berkeley, March 23, 1962

I conceive that a knowledge of books is the basis on which all other knowledge rests.

GEORGE WASHINGTON

I cannot live without books.

THOMAS JEFFERSON, letter to John Adams, June 10, 1815

I have often thought that nothing would do more extensive good at small expense than the establishment of a small circulating library in every county, to consist of a few well-chosen books, to be lent to the people of the country under regulations as would secure their safe return in due time.

THOMAS JEFFERSON, letter to John Wyche, May 19, 1809

I am a part of everything that I have read.

THEODORE ROOSEVELT, 1906

Books cannot be killed by fire. People die, but books never die. No man and no force can abolish memory. No man and no force can put thought in a concentration camp forever. No man and no force can take from the world the books that embody man's eternal fight against tyranny of every kind. In this war, we know, books are weapons. And it is a part of your dedication always to make them weapons for man's freedom.

FRANKLIN D. ROOSEVELT, message to the Booksellers of America, May 6, 1942

Don't join the book burners. Don't think you are going to conceal faults by concealing evidence that they ever existed. Don't be afraid to go in your library and read every book.

> DWIGHT D. EISENHOWER, commencement speech,
> Dartmouth College, Hanover, New Hampshire, June 14, 1953

I am slow to learn and slow to forget that which I have learned. My mind is like a piece of steel—very hard to scratch anything on it, and almost impossible after you get it there to rub it out.

> ABRAHAM LINCOLN, remark to Joshua F. Speed,
> quoted in *Herndon's Lincoln: The True Story of a Great Life*
> by William H. Herndon and Jesse W. Weik

Bigotry is the disease of ignorance, of morbid minds; enthusiasm of the free and buoyant. Education and free discussion are the antidotes of both.

> THOMAS JEFFERSON, letter to John Adams, August 1, 1816

I had not the advantage of a classical education, and no man should, in my judgment, accept a degree he cannot read.

MILLARD FILLMORE, declining an honorary degree from Oxford University, 1855

Upon the subject of education, not presuming to dictate any plan or system respecting it, I can only say that I view it as the most important subject which we as a people can be engaged in.

ABRAHAM LINCOLN, letter to the *Sangamon Journal,* March 9, 1832

Next in importance to freedom and justice is popular education, without which neither freedom nor justice can be permanently sustained.

JAMES A. GARFIELD, letter accepting presidential nomination, 1880

To educate a person in mind and not in morals is to educate a menace to society.

THEODORE ROOSEVELT

What we need now in this nation, more than atomic power, or airpower, or financial, industrial, or even manpower, is brainpower. The dinosaur was bigger and stronger than anyone else—but he was also dumber. And look what happened to him.

JOHN F. KENNEDY, address, Washington, D.C., April 16, 1959

I don't believe I'll ever get credit for anything I do in foreign affairs, no matter how successful it is, because I didn't go to Harvard.

LYNDON B. JOHNSON, comment to columnist Hugh Sidey, quoted in *The Americans* by Alistair Cooke

Not every child has an equal talent or an equal ability or an equal motivation, but they should have the equal right to develop their talent and their ability and their motivation, to make something of themselves.

JOHN F. KENNEDY, radio and television report to the American people on civil rights, June 11, 1963

Education, more than any single force, will mold the citizen of the future. The classroom—not the trench—is the frontier of freedom.

LYNDON B. JOHNSON

Education is about more than making money and mastering technology, even in the twenty-first century. It's about making connections and mastering the complexities of the world. It's about seeing the world as it is and advancing the cause of human dignity.

BILL CLINTON

Chapter 2

Government _and_ Democracy

★ ★ ★

The preservation of the sacred fire of liberty, and the destiny of the republican model of government, are justly considered as deeply, perhaps as finally staked, on the experiment entrusted to the hands of the American people.

GEORGE WASHINGTON, first inaugural address,
April 1789

The republican is the only form of government which is not eternally at open or secret war with the rights of mankind.

THOMAS JEFFERSON, letter to William Hunter, 1790

What is government itself but the greatest of all reflections on human nature? If men were angels, no government would be necessary. If angels were to govern men, neither external nor internal controls on government would be necessary.

JAMES MADISON, *The Federalist Papers*, No. 51,
February 6, 1788

The basis of our government being the opinion of the people, the very first object should be to keep that right; and were it left to me to decide whether we should have a government without newspapers, or newspapers without a government, I should not hesitate a moment to prefer the latter.

THOMAS JEFFERSON, letter to Edward Carrington, January 16, 1787

The judicial power ought to be distinct from both the legislative and executive, and independent upon both, that so it may be a check upon both, as both should be checks upon that.

JOHN ADAMS, "Thoughts on Government," 1776

A wise and frugal Government, which shall restrain men from injuring one another, shall leave them otherwise free to regulate their own pursuits of industry and improvement, and shall not take from the mouth of labor the bread it has earned. This is the sum of good government.

THOMAS JEFFERSON, first inaugural address, March 4, 1801

While all other sciences have advanced, that of government is at a standstill—little better understood, little better practiced now than three or four thousand years ago.

JOHN ADAMS, letter to Thomas Jefferson, July 9, 1813

I am not among those who fear the people. They, and not the rich, are our dependence for continued freedom.

THOMAS JEFFERSON, letter to Samuel Kercheval, July 12, 1816

I know no safe depository of the ultimate powers of society but the people themselves; and if we think them not enlightened enough to exercise their control with a wholesome discretion, the remedy is not to take it from them, but to inform their discretion by education.

THOMAS JEFFERSON, letter to W. C. Jarvis, September 28, 1820

As long as our Government is administered for the good of the people, and is regulated by their will; as long as it secure to us the rights of persons and of property, liberty of conscience and of the press, it will be worth defending.

Andrew Jackson, first inaugural address, March 4, 1829

The spirit of resistance to government is so valuable on certain occasions that I wish it to be always kept alive. It will often be exercised when wrong, but better so than not to be exercised at all.

Thomas Jefferson, letter to Abigail Adams, February 2, 1787

See that the government does not acquire too much power. Keep a check on your rulers. Do this and liberty is safe.

William Henry Harrison

The legitimate object of government is to do for a community of people whatever they need to have done, but cannot do at all, or cannot so well do, for themselves, in their separate and individual capacities.

ABRAHAM LINCOLN, "Fragment on Government,"
July 1, 1854

It is not merely for today, but for all time to come that we should perpetuate for our children's children this great and free government, which we have enjoyed all our lives.

ABRAHAM LINCOLN, speech to 166th Ohio Regiment,
August 22, 1864

Our country offers the most wonderful example of democratic government on a giant scale that the world has ever seen; and the peoples of the world are watching to see whether we succeed or fail.

THEODORE ROOSEVELT

I believe and I say it is true Democratic feeling, that all the measures of Government are directed to the purpose of making the rich richer and the poor poorer.

WILLIAM HENRY HARRISON, speech, October 1, 1840

No government is ever perfect. One of the chief virtues of a democracy, however, is that its defects are always visible and under democratic processes can be pointed out and corrected.

HARRY S. TRUMAN, speech to Congress, March 12, 1947

The experience of democracy is like the experience of life itself—always changing, infinite in its variety, sometimes turbulent and all the more valuable for having been tested by adversity.

JIMMY CARTER, address to the Parliament of India, June 2, 1978

Government is not the solution to our problems;
government is the problem.

> RONALD REAGAN, inaugural address, January 20, 1981

The new rage is to say that the government is the cause
of all our problems, and if only we had no government,
we'd have no problems. I can tell you, that contradicts
evidence, history, and common sense.

> BILL CLINTON, remarks to students at Hillsborough
> Community College, Tampa, Florida, April 3, 1995

If the people cannot trust their government to do the job
for which it exists—to protect them and to promote their
common welfare—all else is lost.

> BARACK OBAMA, speech at University of Nairobi, Kenya,
> August 28, 2006

Chapter 3

Freedom
and Rights

★ ★ ★

Let us dare to read, think, speak and write.

JOHN ADAMS, "Dissertation on the Canon and the Feudal Law," 1765

We are not to expect to be translated from despotism to liberty in a featherbed.

THOMAS JEFFERSON, letter to the Marquis de Lafayette, April 2, 1790

If it be the pleasure of Heaven that my country shall require the poor offering of my life, the victim shall be ready, at the appointed hour of sacrifice, come when that hour may. But while I do live, let me have a country, and that a free country.

JOHN ADAMS, speech, 1776

I believe there are more instances of the abridgment
of the freedom of the people by gradual and silent
encroachments of those in power than by violent and
sudden usurpations.

> JAMES MADISON, address at the Virginia Convention,
> June 16, 1788

To preserve the freedom of the human mind then and
freedom of the press, every spirit should be ready to
devote itself to martyrdom; for as long as we may think
as we will, and speak as we think, the condition of man
will proceed in improvement.

> THOMAS JEFFERSON, letter to William Green Mumford,
> June 18, 1799

Equal and exact justice to all men . . . freedom of
religion, freedom of the press, and freedom of the person
under the protection of the *habeas corpus*; and trial
by juries impartially selected—these principles form
the bright constellation which has gone before us.

> THOMAS JEFFERSON, first inaugural address, March 4, 1801

I have sworn upon the altar of God, eternal hostility against every form of tyranny over the mind of man.

THOMAS JEFFERSON, letter to Benjamin Rush, September 23, 1800

Let us not be unmindful that liberty is power, that the nation blessed with the largest portion of liberty must in proportion to its numbers be the most powerful nation upon earth.

JOHN QUINCY ADAMS, 1821

No man is good enough to govern another man without that other's consent. I say this is the leading principle— the sheet anchor of American republicanism.

ABRAHAM LINCOLN, speech on the Kansas-Nebraska Act, Peoria, Illinois, October 16, 1854

Those who deny freedom to others deserve it not for themselves.

ABRAHAM LINCOLN, letter to H. L. Pierce, April 6, 1859

There is no permanent class of hired laborers among us.
Twenty-five years ago, I was a hired laborer. The hired
laborer of yesterday, labors on his own account to-day;
and will hire others to labor for him to-morrow.

> ABRAHAM LINCOLN, speech, Springfield, Illinois, 1852

Liberty has never come from the government. Liberty
has always come from the subjects of the government.
The history of liberty is the history of resistance.
The history of liberty is a history of the limitations of
governmental power, not the increase of it.

> WOODROW WILSON, speech, New York, New York,
> September 9, 1912

We stand committed to the proposition that freedom
is not a half-and-half affair. If the average citizen is
guaranteed equal opportunity in the polling place, he
must have equal opportunity in the market place.

> FRANKLIN D. ROOSEVELT, speech accepting the Democratic
> nomination for presidency, Democratic National Convention,
> Philadelphia, Pennsylvania, June 27, 1936

In the future days, which we seek to make secure, we look forward to a world founded upon four essential human freedoms. The first is freedom of speech and expression—everywhere in the world. The second is freedom of every person to worship God in his own way—everywhere in the world. The third is freedom from want . . . everywhere in the world. The fourth is freedom from fear . . . anywhere in the world.

FRANKLIN D. ROOSEVELT, Four Freedoms speech, address to Congress, January 6, 1941

Those who would give up essential Liberty to purchase a little temporary Safety deserve neither Liberty nor Safety.

FRANKLIN D. ROOSEVELT, quoting adage used by Benjamin Franklin, Four Freedoms speech, January 6, 1941

Liberty does not make all men perfect nor all society secure. But it has provided more solid progress and happiness and decency for more people than any other philosophy of government in history.

HARRY S. TRUMAN, radio address after signing of the terms of unconditional surrender by Japan, September 1, 1945

Freedom has never been an abstract idea to us here in the United States. It is real and concrete. It means not only political and civil rights; it means much more. It means a society in which man has a fair chance. It means an opportunity to do useful work. It means the right to an education. It means protection against economic hardship.

HARRY S. TRUMAN, address, Independence, Missouri, November 6, 1950

The best way to enhance freedom in other lands is to demonstrate here that our democratic system is worthy of emulation.

JIMMY CARTER, inaugural address, January 20, 1977

We know what works: Freedom works. We know what's right: Freedom is right. We know how to secure a more just and prosperous life for man on earth: through free markets, free speech, free elections and the exercise of free will unhampered by the state.

GEORGE BUSH, inaugural address, January 20, 1989

Our legislators are not sufficiently apprized of the rightful limits of their power; that their true office is to declare and enforce only our natural rights . . . and to take none of them from us. No man has a natural right to commit aggression on the equal rights of another; and this is all from which the laws ought to restrain him . . . and the idea is quite unfounded, that on entering into society we give up any natural right.

THOMAS JEFFERSON, letter to Francis W. Gilmer, June 27, 1816

Freedom means the supremacy of human rights
everywhere. Our support goes to those who struggle
to gain those rights or keep them.

> FRANKLIN D. ROOSEVELT, Four Freedoms speech,
> address to Congress, January 6, 1941

The rights of every man are diminished when the rights
of one man are threatened.

> JOHN F. KENNEDY, on sending the National Guard to ensure
> peaceful integration at the University of Alabama, address
> to the nation, June 11, 1963

Posterity! You will never know how much it cost the
present generation to preserve your freedom! I hope you
will make good use of it! If you do not, I shall repent it in
Heaven that I ever took half the pains to preserve it!

> JOHN ADAMS, letter to Abigail Adams, April 26, 1777

When people talk of the freedom of writing, speaking or thinking I cannot choose but laugh. No such thing ever existed. No such thing now exists; but I hope it will exist. But it must be hundreds of years after you and I shall write and speak no more.

JOHN ADAMS, letter to Thomas Jefferson, July 15, 1818

Chapter 4

Equality, Law, and Justice

★ ★ ★

As mankind becomes more liberal, they will be more able to allow that those who conduct themselves as worthy members of the community are equally entitled to the protection of civil government. I hope ever to see America among the foremost nations in examples of justice and liberality.

GEORGE WASHINGTON, letter to Roman Catholics, 1789

Four score and seven years ago our fathers brought forth on this continent, a new nation, conceived in Liberty, and dedicated to the proposition that all men are created equal.

ABRAHAM LINCOLN, Gettysburg Address, November 19, 1863

I am naturally anti-slavery. If slavery is not wrong, nothing is wrong. I cannot remember when I did not so think, and feel. And yet I have never understood that the Presidency conferred upon me an unrestricted right to act officially upon this judgment and feeling.

ABRAHAM LINCOLN, letter to Albert Hodges, April 4, 1864

Sensible and responsible women do not want to vote. The relative positions to be assumed by man and woman in the working out of our civilization were assigned long ago by a higher intelligence than ours.

GROVER CLEVELAND, 1905

Let the watchwords of all our people be the old familiar watchwords of honesty, decency, fair dealing and common sense.

THEODORE ROOSEVELT, speech, New York State Fair, Syracuse, New York, September 7, 1903

Anti-Semitism is a noxious weed that should be cut out. It has no place in America.

WILLIAM HOWARD TAFT, address to the Anti-Defamation League, Chicago, Illinois, December 23, 1920

We can no longer afford the luxury of a leisurely attack upon prejudice and discrimination. There is much that state and local governments can do in providing positive safeguards for civil rights. But we cannot any longer await the growth of a will to action in the slowest state or the most backward community. Our national government must show the way.

HARRY S. TRUMAN, address to the NAACP, June 29, 1947

Nobody asked me if I was a Catholic when I joined the United States Navy.

JOHN F. KENNEDY, speech addressing his religious affiliation, 1960

No one has been barred on account of his race from fighting or dying for America—there are no "white" or "colored" signs on the foxholes or graveyards of battle.

JOHN F. KENNEDY, message to Congress, June 19, 1963

Finally, it should be clear by now that a nation can be no stronger abroad than she is at home. Only an America which practices what it preaches about equal rights and social justice will be respected by those whose choice affects our future.

JOHN F. KENNEDY, speech prepared for delivery in Dallas, Texas, November 22, 1963

⌒⌒

We have talked long enough in this country about equal rights. We have talked for a hundred years or more. It is time now to write the next chapter, and to write it in the books of law.

LYNDON B. JOHNSON, speech to Congress, November 27, 1963

⌒⌒

As a child, I rode a bus to school each day with the other white students, while the black children walked, and never gave a thought to the lack of equality inherent in the separateness.

JIMMY CARTER, *Keeping Faith: Memoirs of a President*

My grandfather just had a grade-school education. But in that country store he taught me more about equality in the eyes of the Lord than all my professors at Georgetown; more about the intrinsic worth of every individual than all the philosophers at Oxford; and he taught me more about the need for equal justice than all the jurists at Yale Law School.

BILL CLINTON, speech to Democratic National Convention accepting Democratic presidential nomination, July 16, 1992

Laws made by common consent must not be trampled on by individuals.

GEORGE WASHINGTON, letter to Colonel Vanneter, 1781

Ignorance of the law is no excuse, in any country. If it were, the laws would lose their effect, because it can be always pretended.

THOMAS JEFFERSON, letter to M. Limozin, 1787

The execution of the laws is more important than the making of them.

THOMAS JEFFERSON, letter to L'Abbé Arnond, 1789

⌒

Facts are stubborn things; and whatever may be our wishes, our inclinations, or the dictates of our passions, they cannot alter the state of facts and evidence.

JOHN ADAMS, from his defense of the British soldiers in the Boston Massacre Trials, December 1770

⌒

It will be of little avail to the people that the laws are made by men of their own choice if the laws be so voluminous that they cannot be read, or so incoherent that they cannot be understood.

JAMES MADISON

⌒

The great can protect themselves, but the poor and humble require the arm and shield of the law.

ANDREW JACKSON, letter to John Adams, 1821

One great object of the Constitution was to restrain majorities from oppressing minorities or encroaching upon their just rights.

> JAMES K. POLK, inaugural address, March 4, 1845

I know no method to secure the repeal of bad or obnoxious laws so effective as their stringent execution.

> ULYSSES S. GRANT, first inaugural address, March 4, 1869

The law, the will of the majority expressed in orderly, constitutional methods, is the only king to which we bow.

> BENJAMIN HARRISON, speech, Topeka, Kansas,
> October 10, 1890

No man is above the law and no man is below it; nor do we ask any man's permission when we require him to obey it. Obedience to the law is demanded as a right; not asked as a favor.

> THEODORE ROOSEVELT, third State of the Union address,
> December 7, 1903

The Constitution was not made to fit us like a
straitjacket. In its elasticity lies its chief greatness.

WOODROW WILSON, speech, New York, New York,
November 19, 1904

Men speak of natural rights, but I challenge anyone
to show where in nature any rights existed or were
recognized until there was established for their
declaration and protection a duly promulgated body
of corresponding laws.

CALVIN COOLIDGE, acceptance speech, Republican National
Convention, July 27, 1920

The severest justice may not always be the best policy.

ABRAHAM LINCOLN, message to Congress, July 17, 1862

I have always found that mercy bears richer fruits than
strict justice.

ABRAHAM LINCOLN, Washington, D.C., 1865

We can best get justice by doing justice.

> THEODORE ROOSEVELT, speech, "National Duties,"
> September 2, 1901

The friendless, the weak, the victims of prejudice and public excitement are entitled to the same quality of justice and fair play that the rich, the powerful, the well-connected, and the fellow with pull, thinks he can get.

> HARRY S. TRUMAN, speech to the Attorney General's
> Conference, Washington, D.C., February 15, 1950

There is no American right to loot stores, or to burn buildings, or to fire rifles from the rooftops. That is crime—and crime must be dealt with forcefully and swiftly, and certainly—under law.

> LYNDON B. JOHNSON, radio and television speech,
> July 27, 1967

Justice means a man's hope should not be limited by the color of his skin.

> LYNDON B. JOHNSON, State of the Union address,
> January 12, 1966

Chapter 5

Religion
and Morality

★ ★ ★

Religion is as necessary to reason as reason is to religion. The one cannot exist without the other.

GEORGE WASHINGTON, quoted from *The Life of Washington* by James K. Paulding

I never told my own religion, nor scrutinized that of another. I never attempted to make a convert, nor wished to change another's creed. I have ever judged of the religion of others by their lives. . . . For it is in our lives, and not from our words, that our religion must be read.

THOMAS JEFFERSON, letter to Margaret Bayard Smith, August 6, 1816

Every man, conducting himself as a good citizen, and being accountable to God alone for his religious opinions, ought to be protected in worshipping the Deity according to the dictates of his own conscience.

GEORGE WASHINGTON, letter to United Baptist Chamber of Virginia, May, 1789

Government has no Right to hurt a hair of the head of an Atheist for his Opinions. Let him have a care of his Practices.

JOHN ADAMS, letter to John Quincy Adams, June 16, 1816

It does me no injury for my neighbor to say there are twenty Gods, or no God.

THOMAS JEFFERSON, *Notes on the State of Virginia*, 1782

I never will, by any word or act, bow to the shrine of intolerance, or admit a right of inquiry into the religious opinions of others. On the contrary, we are bound, you, I, and everyone, to make common cause, even with error itself, to maintain the common right of freedom of conscience.

THOMAS JEFFERSON, letter to Edward Dowse, April 19, 1803

On Sunday, go to church. Yes, I know all the excuses.
I know that one can worship the Creator and dedicate
oneself to good living in a grove of trees, or by a running
brook, or in one's own house, just as well as in church.
But I also know as a matter of cold fact the average man
does not thus worship or thus dedicate himself. If he
strays away from church, he does not spend his time
in good works or lofty meditation. He looks over the
colored supplement of the newspaper.

> THEODORE ROOSEVELT, quoted in *Ladies Home Journal*,
> October, 1913

Reading, reflection and time have convinced me that the
interests of society require the observation of those moral
precepts only in which all religions agree, for all forbid us
to steal, murder, plunder or bear false witness.

> THOMAS JEFFERSON, letter to James Fishback,
> September 27, 1809

We are firmly convinced . . . that with nations, as with individuals, our interests soundly calculated, will ever be found inseparable from our moral duties.

> THOMAS JEFFERSON, second inaugural address,
> March 4, 1805

Have you ever found in history, one single example of a nation, thoroughly corrupted, that was afterwards restored to virtue? And without virtue there can be no political liberty.

> JOHN ADAMS, letter to Thomas Jefferson,
> December 21, 1819

If I cannot retain my moral influence over a man except by occasionally knocking him down, if that is the only basis upon which he will respect me, then for the sake of his soul I have got occasionally to knock him down.

> WOODROW WILSON, speech, May 15, 1916

A man cannot have character unless he lives within a fundamental system of morals that creates character.

HARRY S. TRUMAN, press conference, 1950

I believe in an America where the separation of church and state is absolute—where no Catholic prelate would tell the President (should he be a Catholic) how to act and no Protestant minister would tell his parishioners for whom to vote—where no church or church school is granted any public funds or political preference—and where no man is denied public office merely because his religion differs from the President who might appoint him or the people who might elect him.

JOHN F. KENNEDY, speech before the Houston Ministerial Association, Houston, Texas, September 12, 1960

America does not need a religious war. It needs reaffirmation of the values that for most of us are rooted in our religious faith.

BILL CLINTON, address, Notre Dame University, September 11, 1992

You cannot divorce religious belief and public service. I've never detected any conflict between God's will and my political duty. If you violate one, you violate the other.

JIMMY CARTER

Modern science has confirmed what ancient faiths have always taught: the most important fact of life is our common humanity. Therefore, we should do more than just tolerate our diversity—we should honor it and celebrate it.

BILL CLINTON

Chapter 6

America

★ ★ ★

The second day of July, 1776, will be the most memorable epoch in the history of America. I am apt to believe that it will be celebrated by succeeding generations as the great anniversary festival. It ought to be commemorated as the day of deliverance, by solemn acts of devotion to God Almighty. It ought to be solemnized with pomp and parade, with shows, games, sports, guns, bells, bonfires, and illuminations, from one end of this continent to the other, from this time forward forevermore.

JOHN ADAMS, second letter to Abigail Adams, July 3, 1776

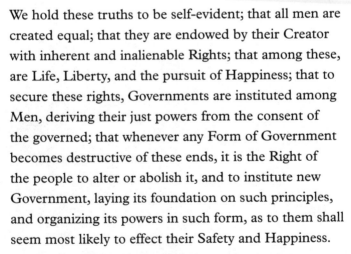

We hold these truths to be self-evident; that all men are created equal; that they are endowed by their Creator with inherent and inalienable Rights; that among these, are Life, Liberty, and the pursuit of Happiness; that to secure these rights, Governments are instituted among Men, deriving their just powers from the consent of the governed; that whenever any Form of Government becomes destructive of these ends, it is the Right of the people to alter or abolish it, and to institute new Government, laying its foundation on such principles, and organizing its powers in such form, as to them shall seem most likely to effect their Safety and Happiness.

The Declaration of Independence, July 4, 1776

America

I always consider the settlement of America with reverence and wonder, as the opening of a grand scene and design in Providence for the illumination of the ignorant, and the emancipation of the slavish part of mankind all over the earth.

> JOHN ADAMS, in his notes for "Dissertation on the Canon and Feudal Law," 1765

They accomplished a revolution which has no parallel in the annals of human society. They reared the fabrics of governments which have no model on the face of the globe. They formed the design of a great Confederacy, which it is incumbent on their successors to improve and perpetuate.

> JAMES MADISON, *The Federalist Papers*, No. 14, November 30, 1787

Citizens, by birth or choice, of a common country,
that country has a right to concentrate your affections.
The name of American, which belongs to you in your
national capacity, must always exalt the just pride of
patriotism more than any appellation derived from local
discriminations.

> GEORGE WASHINGTON, Farewell Address, September 17,
> 1796

There can be no fifty-fifty Americanism in this country.
There is room here for only 100 percent Americanism,
only for those who are Americans and nothing else.

> THEODORE ROOSEVELT, speech, Republican Convention,
> Saratoga, New York, July 18, 1918

It is part of the American character to consider nothing
as desperate, to surmount every difficulty by resolution
and contrivance.

> THOMAS JEFFERSON, letter to Martha Jefferson,
> March 28, 1787

The advice nearest to my heart and deepest in my convictions is that the Union of the States be cherished and perpetuated.

JAMES MADISON, *Advice to My Country,* 1834

All the armies of Europe, Asia and Africa combined, with all the treasure of the earth (our own excepted) in their military chest, with a Bonaparte for a commander, could not, by force, take a drink from the Ohio, or make a track on the Blue Ridge, in a trial of a thousand years.

ABRAHAM LINCOLN, from his address, "The Perpetuation of Our Political Institutions," Springfield, Illinois, January 27, 1837

My purpose is to be, in my action, just and constitutional; and yet practical, in performing the important duty, with which I am charged, of maintaining the unity, and the free principles of our common country.

ABRAHAM LINCOLN, letter to Horatio Seymour, August 7, 1863

Our country has been populated by pioneers, and therefore it has more energy, more enterprise, more expansive power than any other in the whole world.

> THEODORE ROOSEVELT, speech at Minnesota State Fair, September 2, 1901

To waste, to destroy, our natural resources, to skin and exhaust the land instead of using it so as to increase its usefulness, will result in undermining in the days of our children the very prosperity which we ought by right to hand down to them amplified and developed.

> THEODORE ROOSEVELT, State of the Union address, December 3, 1907

America was established not to create wealth but to realize a vision, to realize an ideal—to discover and maintain liberty among men.

> WOODROW WILSON

A man who is good enough to shed his blood for the country is good enough to be given a square deal afterwards.

> THEODORE ROOSEVELT, speech at the Lincoln Monument, Springfield, Illinois, June 4, 1903

I pledge you, I pledge myself, to a new deal for the American people.

> FRANKLIN D. ROOSEVELT, speech to the Democratic Convention in Chicago accepting the presidential nomination, July 2, 1932

This great Nation will endure as it has endured, will revive and will prosper. So, first of all, let me assert my firm belief that we have nothing to fear but fear itself— nameless, unreasoning, unjustified terror which paralyzes needed efforts to convert retreat into advance. In every dark hour of our national life a leadership of frankness and vigor has met with that understanding and support of the people themselves which is essential to victory. I am convinced that you will again give support to leadership in these critical days.

> FRANKLIN D. ROOSEVELT, first inaugural address, March 4, 1933

America is best described by one word, freedom.

> DWIGHT D. EISENHOWER, sixth annual message to
> Congress, January 9, 1958

The torch has been passed to a new generation of Americans—born in this century, tempered by war, disciplined by a hard and bitter peace.

> JOHN F. KENNEDY, inaugural address, January 20, 1961

Let every nation know, whether it wishes us well or ill, that we shall pay any price, bear any burden, meet any hardship, support any friend, oppose any foe to assure the survival and the success of liberty.

> JOHN F. KENNEDY, inaugural address, January 20, 1961

And so, my fellow Americans: ask not what your country can do for you—ask what you can do for your country.

> JOHN F. KENNEDY, inaugural address, January 20, 1961

This administration today, here and now, declares unconditional war on poverty in America. I urge this Congress and all Americans to join with me in that effort. It will not be a short or easy struggle—no single weapon or strategy will suffice—but we shall not rest until that war is won.

> LYNDON B. JOHNSON, State of the Union address,
> January 8, 1964

We become not a melting pot but a beautiful mosaic. Different people, different beliefs, different yearnings, different hopes, different dreams.

> JIMMY CARTER, speech, Pittsburgh, Pennsylvania,
> October 27, 1976

This is America . . . a brilliant diversity spread like stars. Like a thousand points of light in a broad and peaceful sky.

> GEORGE BUSH, inaugural address, January 1989

I refuse to be part of a generation that celebrates
the death of communism abroad with the loss of the
American dream at home.

BILL CLINTON, campaign address, October 3, 1991

There is nothing wrong with America that cannot be
cured with what is right in America.

BILL CLINTON, inaugural address, January 20, 1993

And what a century it has been. America became the
world's mightiest industrial power; saved the world from
tyranny in two world wars and a long cold war; and time
and again, reached out across the globe to millions who,
like us, longed for the blessings of liberty.

BILL CLINTON, second inaugural address, January 20, 1997

I will not forget the wound to our country and those who inflicted it. I will not yield, I will not rest, I will not relent in waging this struggle for freedom and security for the American people.

> GEORGE W. BUSH, speech to joint session of Congress
> wherein President Bush declared the War on Terror,
> September 20, 2001

⌒

If America shows weakness and uncertainty, the world will drift toward tragedy. That will not happen on my watch.

> GEORGE W. BUSH, speech accepting the nomination for
> a second term at the Republican National Convention,
> New York, New York, September 2, 2004

⌒

My heart is filled with love for this country.

> BARACK OBAMA, *The Audacity of Hope*

For we know that our patchwork heritage is a strength, not a weakness. We are a nation of Christians and Muslims, Jews and Hindus, and non-believers. We are shaped by every language and culture, drawn from every end of this Earth; and because we have tasted the bitter swill of civil war and segregation, and emerged from that dark chapter stronger and more united, we cannot help but believe that the old hatreds shall someday pass; that the lines of tribe shall soon dissolve; that as the world grows smaller, our common humanity shall reveal itself; and that America must play its role in ushering in a new era of peace.

BARACK OBAMA, inaugural address, January 20, 2009

I do believe we shall continue to grow, to multiply and prosper until we exhibit an association powerful, wise, and happy beyond what has yet been seen by men.

THOMAS JEFFERSON, letter to John Adams, January 12, 1812

Politics, Politicians,
and Political Parties

Politics is such a torment that I would advise everyone I love not to mix with it.

> THOMAS JEFFERSON, letter to Martha Jefferson Randolph, 1800

I agree with you that in politics the middle way is none at all.

> JOHN ADAMS, letter to Horatio Gates, March 23, 1776

Politics is about economics. People forget that the New Deal was an economic program. A lot of social good came out of it, but it was an economic program.

> BILL CLINTON

The cure for bad politics is the same as the cure for tuberculosis. It is living in the open.

> WOODROW WILSON, speech, Minneapolis, Minnesota, September 18, 1912

I seldom think of politics more than eighteen hours
a day.

LYNDON B. JOHNSON, speech in Texas, 1958

Politics is a very hard game. Winston Churchill once
pointed out that politics is even more difficult than war.
Because in politics you die many times; in war you die
only once.

RICHARD NIXON, letter to Thomas Eagleton, August 2, 1972

In politics, I am growing indifferent. I would like it, if I
could now return to my planting and books at home.

RUTHERFORD B. HAYES, diary entry, April 11, 1876

You and I have formerly seen warm debates and high political passions. But gentlemen of different politics would then speak to each other and separate the business of the Senate from that of society. It is not so now. Men who have been intimate all their lives, cross the streets to avoid meeting, and turn their heads another way, lest they should be obliged to touch their hats. This may do for young men with whom passion is enjoyment. But it is afflicting to peaceable minds. Tranquility is the old man's milk.

THOMAS JEFFERSON, letter to Edward Rutledge, June 24, 1797

If the present Congress errs in too much talking, how can it be otherwise in a body to which the people send 150 lawyers, whose trade it is to question everything, yield nothing, and talk by the hour? That 150 lawyers should do business together ought not to be expected.

THOMAS JEFFERSON, *Autobiography*

It is the duty of the President to propose and it is the privilege of the Congress to dispose.

FRANKLIN D. ROOSEVELT, press conference, July 23, 1937

The passion for office among members of Congress is very great, if not absolutely disreputable, and greatly embarrasses the operations of the Government. They create offices by their own votes and then seek to fill them themselves.

JAMES K. POLK

Nothing brings out the lower traits of human nature like office-seeking. Men of good character and impulses are betrayed by it into all sorts of meanness.

MILLARD FILLMORE

No people is wholly civilized where a distinction is drawn between stealing an office and stealing a purse.

THEODORE ROOSEVELT, speech, Chicago, Illinois,
June 22, 1912

If ever this free people—if this Government itself is ever utterly demoralized, it will come from this human wriggle and struggle for office—a way to live without work; from which nature I am not free myself.

> ABRAHAM LINCOLN, quoted in *Six Months at the White House with Abraham Lincoln* by F. B. Carpenter

One thing our Founding Fathers could not foresee—they were farmers, professional men, businessmen giving of their time and effort to an idea that became a country— was a nation governed by professional politicians who had a vested interest in getting reelected. They probably envisioned a fellow serving a couple of hitches and then looking early forward to getting back to the farm.

> RONALD REAGAN, quoted in *Reagan: The Political Chameleon* by Edmund G. Brown

The most successful politician is he who says what everybody is thinking most often and in the loudest voice.

> THEODORE ROOSEVELT

A good politician has had to be 75 percent ability and 25 percent actor, but I can well see the day when the reverse could be true.

> HARRY S. TRUMAN, quoted in "Images: Roosevelt to Reagan," by Francis X. Clines, *New York Times*, October, 1984

Politicians [are] a set of men who have interests aside from the interests of the people, and who, to say the most of them, are, taken as a mass, at least one long step removed from honest men. I say this with the greater freedom because, being a politician myself, none can regard it as personal.

> ABRAHAM LINCOLN, speech to the Illinois legislature, January 1837

Mothers may still want their favorite sons to grow up to be President, but, according to a famous Gallup poll of some years ago, they do not want them to become politicians in the process.

> JOHN F. KENNEDY, *Profiles in Courage*

Men by their constitutions are naturally divided into two parties: 1. Those who fear and distrust the people, and wish to draw all powers from them into the hands of the higher classes. 2. Those who identify themselves with the people, have confidence in them, cherish and consider them as the most honest and safe, although not the most wise depository of the public interests. . . . Call them . . . Whigs and Tories, Republicans and Federalists, Aristocrats and Democrats, or by whatever name you please, they are the same parties still, and pursue the same object.

THOMAS JEFFERSON, letter to Henry Lee, August 10, 1824

If I could not go to heaven but with a party, I would not go there at all.

THOMAS JEFFERSON, letter to Francis Hopkinson, March 13, 1789

A Republic without parties is a complete anomaly. The histories of all popular governments show how absurd is the idea of their attempting to exist without parties.

FRANKLIN PIERCE

I found a kind of party terrorism pervading and oppressing the minds of our best men.

JAMES A. GARFIELD

Political parties exist to secure responsible government and to execute the will of the people. From these great tasks both of the old parties have turned aside. Instead of instruments to promote the general welfare they have become the tools of corrupt interests, which use them impartially to serve their selfish purposes. Behind the ostensible government sits enthroned an invisible government owing no allegiance and acknowledging no responsibility to the people. To destroy this invisible government, to dissolve the unholy alliance between corrupt business and corrupt politics, is the first task of the statesmanship of the day.

THEODORE ROOSEVELT, "The Progressive Covenant with the People," speech, August 1912

Politics is supposed to be the second oldest profession. I have come to realize that it bears a very close resemblance to the first.

RONALD REAGAN, remarks in Los Angeles, March 2, 1977

I think that in public affairs stupidity is more dangerous than knavery, because harder to fight and dislodge.

WOODROW WILSON, *Fortnightly Review*, February 1913

The more that TV pundits reduce serious debates into silly arguments, and big issues into sound bites, our citizens turn away.

BARACK OBAMA, State of the Union address, January 27, 2010

Chapter 8

The Presidency

★ ★ ★

His character was, in its mass, perfect, in nothing bad, in few points indifferent; and it may truly be said that never did nature and fortune combine more perfectly to make a man great.

> THOMAS JEFFERSON's remark about George Washington
> in letter to Dr. Walter Jones, January 2, 1814

I walk on untrodden ground. There is scarcely any action, whose motives may not be subject to a double interpretation. There is scarcely any part of my conduct which may not hereafter be drawn into precedent.

> GEORGE WASHINGTON, letter to Catharine Sawbridge
> Macaulay Graham, January 9, 1790

All see, and most admire, the glare which hovers round the external trappings of elevated office. To me there is nothing in it, beyond the lustre which may be reflected from its connection with a power of promoting human felicity.

> GEORGE WASHINGTON, letter to Catharine Sawbridge
> Macaulay Graham, January 9, 1790

The Presidency

He seemed to enjoy a triumph over me. Methought
I heard him say, "Ay! I am fairly out and you fairly in!
See which of us will be happiest!"

> JOHN ADAMS, on his reaction to George Washington's
> congratulations to him at Adams's inauguration,
> March 4, 1797

Had I been chosen President again, I am certain I could
not have lived another year.

> JOHN ADAMS, quoted in the *Boston Patriot,* 1809

No man who ever held the office of President would
congratulate a friend on obtaining it. He will make one
man ungrateful, and a hundred men his enemies, for
every office he can bestow.

> JOHN ADAMS, letter to Josiah Quincy, February 14, 1825

The second office of the government is honorable and
easy, the first is but a splendid misery.

> THOMAS JEFFERSON, letter to Elbridge Gerry, May 13, 1797

My country has in its wisdom contrived for me the most insignificant office [the vice presidency] that ever the invention of man contrived or his imagination conceived.

JOHN ADAMS, letter to Abigail Adams, December 19, 1793

I know well that no man will ever bring out of that office the reputation which carries him into it. The honeymoon would be as short in that case as in any other, and its moments of ecstasy would be ransomed by years of torment and hatred.

THOMAS JEFFERSON, letter to Edward Rutledge, December 27, 1796

The danger is that the indulgence and attachments of the people will keep a man in the chair after he becomes a dotard, that reelection through life shall become habitual, and election for life follow that.

THOMAS JEFFERSON, announcement early in his second administration that he would not be a candidate for a third term

The pomp, the turmoil, the bustle and splendor of office, have drawn but deeper sighs for the tranquil and irresponsible occupations of private life.

THOMAS JEFFERSON, letter to inhabitants of Albemarle County, April 3, 1809

Had I been disposed to take advantage of my country a thousand opportunities had before presented themselves, in which I might have made an immense profit, and escaped detection.

JAMES MONROE, letter to General Jackson, July 3, 1825

I can scarcely conceive a more harassing, wearying, teasing condition of existence. It literally renders life burdensome. What retirement will be I cannot realize, but have formed no favorable anticipation. It cannot be worse than this perpetual motion and crazing cares.

JOHN QUINCY ADAMS

As the meeting of Congress approaches, my labors increase. I am engaged preparing for them, and this with my other labors, employs me day and night. I can with truth say mine is a situation of dignified slavery.

ANDREW JACKSON, letter to T. R. J. Chester, November 30, 1829

As to the Presidency, the two happiest days of my life were those of my entrance upon the office and my surrender of it.

MARTIN VAN BUREN

Some folks are silly enough to have formed a plan to make a President of the United States out of this clerk and clodhopper.

WILLIAM HENRY HARRISON

No President who performs his duties faithfully and conscientiously can have any leisure.

JAMES K. POLK, diary entry, September 1, 1847

I prefer to supervise the whole operations of the government myself than entrust the public business to subordinates, and this makes my duties very great.

> JAMES K. POLK, diary entry, December 29, 1848,
> six months before his death at the age of 54, from
> *Polk: The Diary of a President,* edited by Allan Nevins

The idea that I should become President seems to me too visionary to require a serious answer. It has never entered my head, nor is it likely to enter the head of any sane person.

> ZACHARY TAYLOR, letter to his brother, June 11, 1846

If elected, I would not be the mere president of a party—I would endeavor to act independent of party domination and should feel bound to administer the government untrammeled by party schemes.

> ZACHARY TAYLOR, 1848

It is a national disgrace that our Presidents, after having occupied the highest position in the country, should be cast adrift, and, perhaps, be compelled to keep a corner grocery for subsistence.

> MILLARD FILLMORE, letter to a party committee,
> October 12, 1858

It is a relief to feel that no heart but my own can know the personal regret and bitter sorrow over which I have been born to a position so suitable for others rather than desirable for myself.

> FRANKLIN PIERCE, inaugural address, March 4, 1853,
> referring to the recent death of his son, Benjamin

My dear sir, if you are as happy on entering this house as I am leaving, you are a very happy man indeed.

> JAMES BUCHANAN, to his successor Abraham Lincoln, quoted
> in *The Presidents Fact Book* by Roger Matuz

The Presidency, even to the most experienced politicians, is no bed of roses; and General Taylor, like others, found thorns within it. No human being can fill that station and escape censure.

ABRAHAM LINCOLN's eulogy for Zachary Taylor,
Chicago, Illinois, July 25, 1850

I bring to this great work a heart filled with love for my country and an honest desire to do what is right.

ABRAHAM LINCOLN

I have been selected to fill an important office for a brief period, and am now, in your eyes, invested with an influence which will soon pass away; but should my administration prove to be a very wicked one, or what is more probable, a very foolish one, if you, the people, are true to yourselves and the Constitution, there is but little harm I can do, thank God.

ABRAHAM LINCOLN, speech, Lawrenceburg, Indiana,
February 28, 1861

You have little idea of the terrible weight of care and sense of responsibility of this office of mine. Schenck, if to be at the head of Hell is as hard as what I have to undergo here, I could find it in my heart to pity Satan himself.

> ABRAHAM LINCOLN, remark to General Robert E. Schenck,
> from *Reminiscences of Abraham Lincoln* edited by Allen T. Rice

It was my fortune, or misfortune, to be called to the office of Chief Executive without any previous political training.

> ULYSSES S. GRANT, State of the Union address,
> December 5, 1876

Well I am heartily tired of this life of bondage, responsibility and toil.

> RUTHERFORD B. HAYES, diary entry, June 6, 1879

I am casting about me to find someone who will help to enliven the solitude which surrounds the Presidency. The unfortunate incumbent of that office is the most isolated man in America.

JAMES A. GARFIELD, letter to John Hay, 1881

I may be President of the United States, but my private life is nobody's damn business.

CHESTER A. ARTHUR

Franklin, I hope you never become President.

GROVER CLEVELAND, comment to the boy Franklin D. Roosevelt, quoted in *The American Treasury, 1455–1955* edited by Clifton Fadiman

There is a great sense of loneliness in the discharge of high public duties. The moment of decision is one of isolation.

BENJAMIN HARRISON

I have had enough of it, heaven knows, I have had responsibilities enough to kill any man.

WILLIAM McKINLEY

I have a very definite philosophy about the Presidency. I think it should be a very powerful office, and I think the President should be a very strong man who uses without hesitation every power that the position yields; but because of this fact I believe that he should be sharply watched by the people [and] held to a strict accountability by them.

THEODORE ROOSEVELT, letter to Henry Cabot Lodge, July 19, 1908

No other President ever enjoyed the Presidency as I did.

THEODORE ROOSEVELT, letter to G. O. Trevelyan, September 10, 1909

The best executive is one who has sense enough to pick good people to do what he wants done, and self-restraint enough to keep from meddling with them while they do it.

THEODORE ROOSEVELT

I have got such a bully pulpit!

THEODORE ROOSEVELT, comment to George Haven Putnam, recalled by Putnam at Roosevelt eulogy, the Century Club, New York, New York, 1919

I'll be glad to be going—this is the loneliest place in the world.

WILLIAM HOWARD TAFT, comment to Woodrow Wilson at Wilson's inauguration, Washington, D.C., March 4, 1913

The President is at liberty, both in law and conscience, to be as big a man as he can.

WOODROW WILSON, 1907

The presidential office is not a rosewater affair. This is an office in which a man must put on his war paint.

> WOODROW WILSON, *Woodrow Wilson: Life and Letters*
> by Ray Stannard Baker

[The presidency demands:] the constitution of an athlete, the patience of a mother, and the endurance of an early Christian.

> WOODROW WILSON, quoted in *Presidential Wit from
> Washington to Johnson* edited by Bill Adler

My God, this is a hell of a job! I have no trouble with my enemies. I can take care of my enemies all right. But my damn friends, my goddamn friends. . . . They're the ones that keep me walking the floor nights!

> WARREN G. HARDING, comment to William Allen White,
> reported in White's *Autobiography*

In the discharge of the duties of the office there is one rule of action more important than all others. It consists of never doing anything that someone else can do for you.

CALVIN COOLIDGE, *Autobiography*

It is preeminently a place of moral leadership.

FRANKLIN D. ROOSEVELT, quoted by Anne O'Hare McCormick in *New York Times,* September 11, 1932

The buck stops here.

sign on HARRY S. TRUMAN's desk

Within the first few months I discovered that being a President is like riding a tiger. A man has to keep on riding or be swallowed. . . . I never felt that I could let up for a single moment.

HARRY S. TRUMAN, *Years of Trial and Hope*

All the President is, is a glorified public relations man who spends his time flattering, kissing, and kicking people to get them to do what they are supposed to do anyway.

> HARRY S. TRUMAN, letter to his sister, Mary Jane Truman, November 14, 1947

A short time after the new President takes his oath of office, I will be on the train going back to Independence, Missouri. I will once again be a plain, private citizen of this great Republic. . . . It is a good object lesson in democracy. I am very proud of it.

> HARRY S. TRUMAN, Farewell Address, January 15, 1953

When you get to be President, there are all those things, the honors, the twenty-one gun salutes, all those things. You have to remember it isn't for you. It's for the Presidency.

> HARRY S. TRUMAN, quoted in *Plain Speaking: An Oral Biography of Harry S. Truman* by Merle Miller

A sense of humor is part of the art of leadership,
of getting along with people, of getting things done.

DWIGHT D. EISENHOWER

⁓

If ever for a second time [1956] I should show any signs
of yielding to persuasion to run, please call in the
psychiatrist—or even better, the sheriff.

DWIGHT D. EISENHOWER, comment to Milton Eisenhower,
December 11, 1953

⁓

When we got into office, the thing that surprised me
most was to find that things were just as bad as we'd
been saying they were.

JOHN F. KENNEDY, speech at his forty-fourth birthday
celebration, May 27, 1961

With American sons in the fields far away, with America's future under challenge right here at home, with our hopes and the world's hopes for peace in the balance every day, I do not believe that I should devote an hour or a day of my time to any personal partisan causes or to any duties other than the awesome duties of this office—the Presidency of your country. Accordingly, I shall not seek, and I will not accept, the nomination of my party for another term as your president.

LYNDON B. JOHNSON, address, March 31, 1968

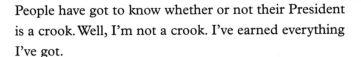

People have got to know whether or not their President is a crook. Well, I'm not a crook. I've earned everything I've got.

RICHARD M. NIXON, news conference, November 17, 1973

Throughout the long and difficult period of Watergate, I have felt it was my duty to persevere, to make every possible effort to complete the term of office to which you elected me. In the past few days, however, it has become evident to me that I no longer have a strong enough political base in the Congress to justify continuing that effort. . . . To leave office before my term is completed is abhorrent to every instinct in my body. But as President, I must put the interests of America first. . . . Therefore I shall resign the presidency effective noon tomorrow.

> RICHARD M. NIXON, address to the nation, August 8, 1974

Our long national nightmare is over.

> GERALD R. FORD, remark upon taking the oath of office, August 9, 1974

I am acutely aware that you have not elected me as your President by your ballots, and so I ask you to confirm me as your President with your prayers.

GERALD R. FORD, inaugural address, August 9, 1974

I have always looked on the Presidency of the United States with reverence and awe, and I still do. But recently I have begun to realize that the President is just a human being.

JIMMY CARTER

There have been times in this office when I have wondered how you could do this job if you hadn't been an actor.

RONALD REAGAN, in response to question during a televised interview with David Brinkley wherein Brinkley asked the president if anything he'd learned as an actor had helped him during his presidency, December 22, 1988

Some see leadership as high drama and the sound of trumpets calling. And sometimes it is that. But I see history as a book with many pages—and each day we fill a page with acts of hopefulness and meaning.

> GEORGE BUSH, inaugural address, January 20, 1989

Don't let [the White House] fool you. It's the crown jewel of the federal prison system.

> BILL CLINTON, remark to his political advisers while touring the White House shortly after his inauguration, from "The Education of a President," by Sidney Blumenthal in the *New Yorker*, January 24, 1994

I'm not going to be the guy who promises something he can't deliver. I don't believe in "ready, fire, aim."

> GEORGE W. BUSH

Transparency and the rule of law will be the touchstones of this presidency.

> BARACK OBAMA, at the signing of executive orders on the first full day of his presidency, January 21, 2009

Chapter 9

Peace, War,
and Foreign Relations

★ ★ ★

There is nothing so likely to produce peace as to be well prepared to meet an enemy.

GEORGE WASHINGTON, letter to Elbridge Gerry,
January 29, 1780

So strong is this propensity of mankind to fall
into mutual animosities, that where no substantial
occasion presents itself, the most frivolous and
fanciful distinctions have been sufficient to kindle
their unfriendly passions and excite their most violent
conflicts.

JAMES MADISON, *The Federalist Papers,* No. 10,
November 23, 1787

I love peace, and I am anxious that we should give the
world still another useful lesson, by showing to them
other modes of punishing injuries than by war, which is
as much a punishment to the punisher as to the sufferer.

THOMAS JEFFERSON, letter to Tench Coxe, May 1, 1794

Peace with all the world is my sincere wish. I am sure it is our true policy, and am persuaded it is the ardent desire of the government.

> GEORGE WASHINGTON, letter to Reverend Jonathan Boucher, August 15, 1798

Peace, above all things, is to be desired, but blood must sometimes be spilled to obtain it on equable and lasting terms.

> ANDREW JACKSON

To avoid entangling alliances has been a maxim of our policy ever since the days of Washington, and its wisdom no one will attempt to dispute.

> JAMES BUCHANAN

With malice toward none; with charity for all; with firmness in the right, as God gives us to see the right, let us strive on to finish the work we are in; to bind up the nation's wounds; to care for him who shall have borne the battle, and for his widow, and his orphan—to do all which may achieve and cherish a just and lasting peace among ourselves, and with all nations.

ABRAHAM LINCOLN, second inaugural address, March 4, 1865

The war is over—the rebels are our countrymen again.

ULYSSES S. GRANT, stopping his men from cheering after Lee's surrender at Appomattox, April 9, 1865

With capability for war on land and on sea unexcelled by any nation in the world, we are smitten by the love of peace.

BENJAMIN HARRISON, speech, San Francisco, California, May 1891

Peace is normally a great good, and normally it coincides with righteousness, but it is righteousness and not peace which should bind the conscience of a nation as it should bind the conscience of an individual; and neither a nation nor an individual can surrender conscience to another's keeping.

> THEODORE ROOSEVELT, sixth annual message to Congress, December 4, 1906

There never has been—there never can be—successful compromise between good and evil. Only total victory can reward the champions of tolerance and decency and freedom and faith.

> FRANKLIN D. ROOSEVELT, State of the Union address, Washington, D.C., 1942

I want peace and I'm willing to fight for it.

> HARRY S. TRUMAN, diary entry, May 22, 1945, quoted in *Off the Record* by Robert H. Ferrell

No man should think that peace comes easily. Peace does not come by merely wanting it, or shouting for it, or marching down Main Street for it. Peace is built brick by brick, mortared by the stubborn effort and the total energy and imagination of able and dedicated men. And it is built in the living faith that, in the end, man can and will master his own destiny.

> LYNDON B. JOHNSON, *The Vantage Point: Perspectives of the Presidency, 1963–1969*

Peace is a daily, a weekly, a monthly process, gradually changing opinions, slowly eroding old barriers, quietly building new structures. And however undramatic the pursuit of peace, that pursuit must go on.

> JOHN F. KENNEDY, speech at United Nations, September 1963

In this age when there can be no losers in peace and no victors in war, we must recognize the obligation to match national strength with national restraint.

> LYNDON B. JOHNSON, addressing a joint session of Congress, November 27, 1963

In times of peace the people look most to their representatives; but in war, to the executive solely.

> THOMAS JEFFERSON, letter to Caesar A. Rodney,
> February 10, 1810

Be it remembered, then, that there are tumults, seditions, popular commotions, insurrections, and civil wars, upon just occasions as well as unjust.

> JOHN ADAMS, *Novanglus Papers*, 1774

A President can declare war and can conclude peace without being hurled from his chair.

> JOHN ADAMS, letter to W. S. Smith, February 22, 1815

The spirit of this country is totally adverse to a large military force.

> THOMAS JEFFERSON, letter to Chandler Price,
> February 28, 1807

The right of self-defense never ceases. It is among the most sacred, and alike necessary to nations and to individuals.

JAMES MONROE

Overgrown military establishments are under any form of government inauspicious to liberty, and are to be regarded as particularly hostile to republican liberty.

GEORGE WASHINGTON, Farewell Address, September 17, 1796

The art of war is simple enough. Find out where your enemy is. Get at him as soon as you can. Strike him as hard as you can, and keep moving on.

ULYSSES S. GRANT, statement to John Hill Brinton at the start of the Tennessee River Campaign, 1862, quoted in *Personal Memoirs of John H. Brinton, Major and Surgeon U.S.V., 1861–1865*

Old men declare war. But it is the youth that must fight and die.

HERBERT HOOVER

I have seen war. I have seen war on land and sea. I have seen blood running from the wounded. I have seen men coughing out their gassed lungs. I have seen the dead in the mud. I have seen cities destroyed. I have seen two hundred limping, exhausted men come out of line— the survivors of a regiment of one thousand that went forward forty-eight hours before. I have seen children starving. I have seen the agony of mothers and wives. I hate war.

FRANKLIN D. ROOSEVELT, speech at Chautauqua, New York, August 14, 1936

I hate war as only a soldier who has lived it can, only as one who has seen its brutality, its futility, and its stupidity.

DWIGHT D. EISENHOWER, speech, Ottawa, Canada, January 10, 1956

Those who make peaceful revolution impossible will make violent revolution inevitable.

JOHN F. KENNEDY, speech to Latin American diplomats, March 12, 1962

Let us never negotiate out of fear. But let us never fear to negotiate.

JOHN F. KENNEDY, inaugural address, January 20, 1961

Mankind must put an end to war or war will put an end to mankind.

JOHN F. KENNEDY, address to the United Nations, September 25, 1961

Nations do not mistrust each other because they are armed; they are armed because they mistrust each other.

RONALD REAGAN, address to the United Nations, New York, New York, September 22, 1986

Let terrorists beware that when the rules of international behavior are violated, our policy will be one of swift and effective retribution.

> RONALD REAGAN, speech, Washington, D.C., January 27, 1981

Terrorist attacks can shake the foundations of our biggest buildings, but they cannot touch the foundation of America. These acts shattered steel, but they cannot dent the steel of American resolve.

> GEORGE W. BUSH, address to the nation, September 11, 2001

Every nation, in every region, now has a decision to make. Either you are with us, or you are with the terrorists.

> GEORGE W. BUSH, addressing a joint session of Congress and the American people, September 20, 2001

Where the stakes are the highest, in the war on terror, we cannot possibly succeed without extraordinary international cooperation. Effective international police actions require the highest degree of intelligence sharing, planning and collaborative enforcement.

> BARACK OBAMA, speech, Chicago Council on Global Affairs, July 12, 2004

Responsibility and leadership in the 21st century demand more. In an era when our destiny is shared, power is no longer a zero sum game. No one nation can or should try to dominate another nation. No world order that elevates one nation or group of people over another will succeed. No balance of power among nations will hold.

> BARACK OBAMA, speech at United Nations, September 27, 2009

The Economy, Business, Labor, *and* Wealth

A wise and frugal Government, which shall restrain men from injuring one another, shall leave them otherwise free to regulate their own pursuits of industry and improvement, and shall not take from the mouth of labor the bread it has earned. This is the sum of good government.

THOMAS JEFFERSON, first inaugural address, March 4, 1801

Agriculture, manufactures, commerce, and navigation, the four pillars of our prosperity, are the most thriving when left to individual enterprise.

THOMAS JEFFERSON, first annual message to Congress, December 8, 1801

Indebtedness cannot be lessened by borrowing more money, or by changing the form of the debt.

MARTIN VAN BUREN, President's Message, December 1839

The truth is, we are all caught in a great economic system which is heartless.

> WOODROW WILSON, *The New Freedom*

If our institutions and our cities and states and nation only spent the money they had in hand, we wouldn't be in the mess we are today.

> CALVIN COOLIDGE, remark to Stanley King, 1930

Nothing is easier than spending public money. It does not appear to belong to anybody. The temptation is overwhelming to bestow it on somebody.

> CALVIN COOLIDGE, quoted in *Reader's Digest*, June 1960

No taxes can be devised which are not more or less inconvenient and unpleasant.

> GEORGE WASHINGTON, Farewell Address, September 17, 1796

The revenue of the country, levied almost insensibly to the taxpayer, goes on from year to year, increasing beyond either the interests or the prospective wants of the government.

FRANKLIN PIERCE, first annual address, December 5, 1853

True democracy . . . seeks to lighten the burdens of life in every home and to take from the citizen for the cost of government the lowest possible tribute.

GROVER CLEVELAND, speech at the Democratic Club, New York, New York, April 1889

Here is my principle: Taxes shall be levied according to the ability to pay. That is the only American principle.

FRANKLIN D. ROOSEVELT, campaign address, Worcester, Massachusetts, October 21, 1936

The present tax structure is a disgrace to this country; it's just a welfare program for the rich.

> JIMMY CARTER, first Ford-Carter debate,
> Philadelphia, Pennsylvania, September 23, 1976

Read my lips, no new taxes.

> GEORGE BUSH, acceptance speech, Republican National
> Convention, August 18, 1988

It is true that I want to roll back the Bush tax cuts on the very wealthiest Americans and go back to the rate that they paid under Bill Clinton. John McCain calls that socialism. What he forgets, conveniently, is that just a few years ago, he himself said those Bush tax cuts were irresponsible. He said he couldn't in good conscience support tax cuts where the benefit went to the wealthy at the expense of middle-class Americans who most need the tax relief. That's his quote. Well, he was right then, and I am right now.

> BARACK OBAMA, campaign speech, Tampa, Florida,
> October 20, 2009

The chief business of the American people is business. They are profoundly concerned with producing, buying, selling, investing, and prospering in the world.

> CALVIN COOLIDGE, speech, Society of American Newspaper Editors, Washington, D.C., January 1925

These capitalists generally act harmoniously and in concert, to fleece the people.

> ABRAHAM LINCOLN, speech in Illinois legislature, January 1837

We demand that big business give people a square deal; in return we must insist that when any one engaged in big business honestly endeavors to do right, he shall himself be given a square deal.

> THEODORE ROOSEVELT, writing on the Taft administration's attempts to dissolve the Steel Trust, *Autobiography*

Nothing will contribute so much to American industrial stability and add so much to American industrial happiness as the abolition of the twelve-hour working day and the seven-day working week.

> WARREN G. HARDING, speech to steel leaders, Washington, D.C., May 1923

It is just as important that business keep out of government as that government keep out of business.

> HERBERT HOOVER, speech, October 22, 1928

This concentration of wealth and power has been built upon other people's money, other people's business, other people's labor. Under this concentration independent business was allowed to exist only by sufferance. It has been a menace to the social system as well as to the economic system which we call American democracy.

> FRANKLIN D. ROOSEVELT, campaign speech, October 14, 1936

It's a recession when your neighbor loses his job; it's a depression when you lose yours.

HARRY S. TRUMAN, quoted in *The Observer*, April 13, 1958

Today too many Americans in country clubs and fashionable resorts are repeating, like parrots, the phrase "labor must be kept in its place." It is time that all Americans realize that the place of labor is side by side with the businessman and with the farmer, and not one degree lower.

HARRY S. TRUMAN, Labor Day address, Detroit, Michigan, September 6, 1948

A truly American sentiment recognizes the dignity of labor and the fact that honor lies in honest toil.

GROVER CLEVELAND

I pity the man who wants a coat so cheap that the
man or woman who produces the cloth will starve
in the process.

BENJAMIN HARRISON

I believe in an America where every man or woman
who wants to find work can find work—where a growing economy provides new jobs and new markets for a
growing nation without inflating the consumer's prices
beyond the reach of his family budget.

JOHN F. KENNEDY, speech, Philadelphia, Pennsylvania,
October 31, 1960

No dramatic challenge is more crucial than providing
stable, permanent jobs for all Americans who want
to work.

RONALD REAGAN, State of the Union address,
January 25, 1983

Wealth can only be accumulated by the earnings of
industry and the savings of frugality.

JOHN TYLER

That some should be rich shows that others may become
rich, and, hence, is just encouragement to industry and
enterprise.

ABRAHAM LINCOLN, reply to the New York Workingman's
Association, March 21, 1864

Poverty is uncomfortable; but nine times out of ten
the best thing that can happen to a young man is to be
tossed overboard and compelled to sink or swim.

JAMES A. GARFIELD

Focusing your life solely on making a buck shows a certain poverty of ambition. It asks too little of yourself. Because it's only when you hitch your wagon to something larger than yourself that you realize your true potential.

> BARACK OBAMA, commencement address at Knox College, June 4, 2005

Chapter 11

Family *and* Friendship

The happiest moments of my life have been the few which I have passed at home in the bosom of my family.

THOMAS JEFFERSON, letter to Francis Willis, Jr., April 18, 1790

As much as I converse with sages and heroes, they have very little of my love or admiration. I long for rural and domestic scenes, for the warbling of birds and the prattle of my children.

JOHN ADAMS, letter to Abigail Adams, March 16, 1777

I had rather be shut up in a very modest cottage with my books, my family and a few old friends, dining on simple bacon, and letting the world roll on as it liked, than to occupy the most splendid post, which any human power can give.

THOMAS JEFFERSON, letter to Alexander Donald, February 7, 1788

Be courteous to all, but intimate with few; and let those few be well tried before you give them your confidence. True friendship is a plant of slow growth, and must undergo and withstand the shocks of adversity before it is entitled to the appellation.

> GEORGE WASHINGTON, letter to his nephew,
> Bushrod Washington, January 15, 1783

A letter from you calls up recollections very dear to my mind. It carries me back to the times when, beset with difficulties and dangers, we were fellow laborers in the same cause, struggling with what is most valuable to man, his right of self-government. Laboring always at the same oar, with some wave ever ahead threatening to overwhelm us and yet passing under our bark, we knew not how, we rode through the storm with heart and hand, and made a happy port.

> THOMAS JEFFERSON, letter to John Adams, January 21, 1812,
> sent in response to a note from Adams. The two had not
> spoken for twelve years after their bitterly waged presidential
> election in 1800. With this letter, their friendship was renewed
> and they shared a rich correspondence until their deaths,
> within hours of one another, on July 4, 1826.

You know little of Andrew Jackson if you suppose him capable of consenting to . . . a humiliation of his friends by his enemies.

> ANDREW JACKSON, rejecting Martin Van Buren's resignation as secretary of state, 1831

All the friends that I loved and wanted to reward are dead, and all the enemies that I hated and I had marked out for punishment are turned to my friends.

> JAMES BUCHANAN, on achieving the presidency at the age of sixty-five

The friend in my adversity I shall always cherish most. I can better trust those who helped to relieve the gloom of my dark hours than those who are so ready to enjoy with me the sunshine of my prosperity.

> ULYSSES S. GRANT

There never was a woman like her. She was gentle as a dove and brave as a lioness. . . . The memory of my mother and her teachings were, after all, the only capital I had to start life with, and on that capital I have made my way.

ANDREW JACKSON

She was the cornerstone of our family and a woman of extraordinary accomplishment, strength and humility. She was the person who encouraged and allowed us to take chances.

BARACK OBAMA, on the death of his eighty-six-year-old grandmother, Madelyn Dunham, in 2008

In this troublesome world, we are never quite satisfied. When you were here, I thought you hindered me some in attending to business; but now, having nothing but business—no variety—it has grown exceedingly tasteless to me. I hate to sit down and direct documents, and I hate to stay in this old room by myself.

ABRAHAM LINCOLN, letter to Mary Todd Lincoln,
April 16, 1848, written to her from Washington, D.C.,
while she and their two boys were visiting family in Kentucky

Sometimes I think that I get far less leisure than any other mortal and have far less of the enjoyments of life. It is a fearful price to pay for a little publicity—to be obliged to throw away all the dear pleasures of home and family just at a time when enjoyment has the keenest relish.

JAMES A. GARFIELD, February 1864

I love you, precious, with all my heart and to know that you love me means my life. How often I have thought about the immeasurable joy that will be ours some day. How lucky our children will be to have a mother like you.

GEORGE BUSH, letter to Barbara Pierce, December 12, 1943, quoted in *All the Best, George Bush*

A man not honorable in his marital relations is not usually honorable in any other.

HARRY S. TRUMAN, 1931

What men owe to the love and help of good women can never be told.

CALVIN COOLIDGE, *Autobiography,*

I don't know what history will say about me, but I know it will say that Pat Nixon was a truly wonderful woman.

RICHARD M. NIXON, quoted in *Presidential Wives* by Paul F. Boller

Only two things are necessary to keep one's wife happy. One is to let her think she is having her own way, and the other, to let her have it.

LYNDON B. JOHNSON

There is very seldom a decision that I make that I don't discuss with her [Rosalynn Carter], tell her my opinion and seek her advice. . . . On matters where her knowledge is equal to mine, she prevails most of the time.

JIMMY CARTER, quoted in *Presidential Wives* by Paul F. Boller

I have spent many hours of my life giving speeches and expressing my opinions. But it is almost impossible for me to express fully how deeply I love Nancy and how much she has filled my life.

RONALD REAGAN, *An American Life*

And I would not be standing here tonight without the unyielding support of my best friend for the last sixteen years . . . the rock of our family, the love of my life, the nation's next first lady . . . Michelle Obama.

> BARACK OBAMA, speech upon winning the presidential
> election, Chicago, Illinois, November 4, 2008

⌒

I miss you all dreadfully, and the house feels big and lonely and full of echoes with nobody but me in it; and I do not hear any small scamps running up and down the hall just as hard as they can; or hear their voices while I am dressing; or suddenly look out through the windows of the office at the tennis ground and see them racing over it or playing in the sand-box. I love you very much.

> THEODORE ROOSEVELT, letter to his son Quentin,
> written from the White House on April 1, 1906,
> quoted in *A Bully Father* by Joan Paterson Kerr

⌒

Children and dogs are as necessary to the welfare of this country as Wall Street and the railroads.

> HARRY S. TRUMAN, remark to National Conference
> of Family Life, May 6, 1948

Our little girl was a healthy six pounds, one and three quarters ounces, and she cried on cue. While Hillary was in the recovery room, I carried Chelsea out to Mother and anyone else who was available to see the world's most wonderful baby. I talked to her and sang to her. I never wanted that night to end. At last I was a father. Despite my love for politics and government and my growing ambitions, I knew then that being a father was the most important job I'd ever have. Thanks to Hillary and Chelsea, it also turned out to be the most rewarding.

BILL CLINTON, *My Life*

I can be president of the United States or I can control Alice. I cannot possibly do both.

THEODORE ROOSEVELT, in response to a dignitary who inquired about his daughter's unruly behavior, quoted in *Hail to the Chiefs: My Life and Times with Six Presidents* by Ruth Shick Montgomery

It is my pleasure that my children are free and happy, and unrestrained by parental tyranny. Love is the chain whereby to bind a child to its parents.

ABRAHAM LINCOLN, frequent remark to Mary Todd Lincoln, quoted in *Herndon's Lincoln* by William H. Herndon and Jesse W. Weik

Chapter 12

Presidential Quips
and Gaffes

This is the most extraordinary collection of talent, of human knowledge, that has ever been gathered at the White House, with the possible exception of when Thomas Jefferson dined alone.

JOHN F. KENNEDY, remarks at dinner for Nobel Prize winners at the White House, April 1962

If you don't have a sense of humor, you're in a hell of a fix when you are President of the United States.

HARRY S. TRUMAN, *Quote* magazine, October 5, 1947

Washington, D.C. is twelve square miles bordered by reality.

ANDREW JOHNSON

Washington is a city of northern charm and southern efficiency.

JOHN F. KENNEDY

If the general had known how big a funeral he would have had, he would have died years ago.

> ABRAHAM LINCOLN, remark to David R. Locke about
> a recently deceased politician known for his great vanity,
> from *Lincoln Talks: A Biography in Anecdote*
> edited by Emanuel Hertz

If you want a friend in Washington, get a dog.

> HARRY S. TRUMAN

I've been criticized by quite a few people for making my brother Bobby attorney general. They didn't realize that I had a very good reason for that appointment. Bobby wants to practice law, and I thought he ought to get a little experience first.

> JOHN F. KENNEDY, remark at press conference,
> quoted in *The Uncommon Wisdom of JKF*
> edited by Bill Adler and Tom Folsom

An amazing invention—but who would ever want to use one?

> RUTHERFORD B. HAYES, commenting about Alexander
> Graham Bell's invention after making a call from Washington
> to Pennsylvania, quoted in *Words from Our Presidents*
> edited by Trevor Hunt

A man who never has gone to school may steal from a freight car, but if he has a university education, he may steal from the whole railroad.

> THEODORE ROOSEVELT, quoted in *Art of Communicating
> Ideas* by William Joseph Grace

There are only two occasions when Americans respect privacy, especially in presidents. Those are prayer and fishing.

> HERBERT HOOVER, *New York Herald Tribune,* May 19, 1947

Being president is like being a jackass in a hailstorm. There's nothing to do but to stand there and take it.

> LYNDON JOHNSON

Well, when the President does it that means that it is not illegal.

> RICHARD M. NIXON, televised interview with David Frost, May 20, 1977, referring to the so-called Huston plan and President Nixon's views on presidential authority

I have orders to be awakened at any time in the case of a national emergency, even if I'm in a cabinet meeting.

> RONALD REAGAN

I was under medication when I made the decision to burn the tapes.

> RICHARD M. NIXON, quoted in *Words from Our Presidents* edited by Trevor Hunt

If you can't convince them, confuse them.

> HARRY S. TRUMAN

It is clear our nation is reliant upon big foreign oil. More and more of our imports come from overseas.

GEORGE W. BUSH

You can put lipstick on a pig. It's still a pig.

BARACK OBAMA, September 2008

Tip O'Neill once asked me how I keep myself looking so young for the cameras. I told him I have a good makeup team—the same people who've been repairing the Statue of Liberty.

RONALD REAGAN, 1986, quoted in *The Reagan Wit* edited by Bill Adler and Bill Adler, Jr.

I'm a conservative, but I'm not a nut about it.

GEORGE BUSH

Being president is like running a cemetery; you've got a lot of people under you and nobody's listening.

BILL CLINTON, speech, Galesburg, Illinois, January 1995

To those of you who received honors, awards and distinctions, I say, well done. And to the "C" students, I say: you too can be president.

GEORGE W. BUSH

Contrary to the rumors you have heard, I was not born in a manger. I was actually born on Krypton and sent here by my father Jor-El to save the Planet Earth.

BARACK OBAMA, charity event, October 2008

Chapter 13

Wisdom
of the Presidents

★ ★ ★

Labor to keep alive in your breast that little spark of celestial fire called conscience.

> favorite quote of GEORGE WASHINGTON's
> from *Rules of Civility and Decent Behavior,* which he
> copied into his school book when he was sixteen

Take more pleasure in giving what is best to another than in having it yourself, and then all the world will love you, and I more than all the world.

> THOMAS JEFFERSON, letter to his daughter, Mary Jefferson,
> April 11, 1790

It is neither wealth nor splendor, but tranquility and occupation, which give happiness.

> THOMAS JEFFERSON, letter to Mrs. A. S. Marks, 1788

Any man worth his salt will stick up for what he believes right, but it takes a slightly better man to acknowledge instantly and without reservation that he is in error.

> ANDREW JACKSON

No tendency is quite so strong in human nature as the desire to lay down rules of conduct for other people.

> WILLIAM HOWARD TAFT, quoted in *Mr. Capone*
> by Robert J. Schoenberg

⌒

Take time to deliberate; but when the time for action arrives, stop thinking and go in.

> ANDREW JACKSON

⌒

Speak softly and carry a big stick; you will go far.

> THEODORE ROOSEVELT, quoting an old adage in a speech,
> Chicago, April 3, 1903

⌒

If you can't stand the heat you better get out of the kitchen.

> HARRY S. TRUMAN, address to the Aero Club of Washington,
> December 27, 1952, quoting a colleague from his time as a
> county judge

Never go out to meet trouble. If you just sit still, nine cases out of ten, someone will intercept it before it reaches you.

CALVIN COOLIDGE

You let a bully come into your front yard, and the next day he'll be on your porch.

LYNDON B. JOHNSON, quoted in *Time*, April 1964

One cool judgment is worth a thousand hasty counsels. The thing to do is supply light and not heat.

WOODROW WILSON

Patience and perseverance have a magical effect before which difficulties disappear and obstacles vanish.

JOHN QUINCY ADAMS

Popularity, I have always thought, may aptly be compared to a coquette—the more you woo her, the more apt is she to elude your embrace.

JOHN TYLER

Give about two [hours], every day, to exercise; for health must not be sacrificed to learning. A strong body makes the mind strong.

THOMAS JEFFERSON, letter to Peter Carr, August 19, 1785

I think we ought to concern ourselves with making sure that our children are fit, that they are concerned with being energetic—that they use their young years not merely as spectators but as participants in life.

JOHN F. KENNEDY, interview, Washington, D.C., January 31, 1961

When you play, play hard. When you work, don't play at all.

THEODORE ROOSEVELT

A mind always employed is always happy. This is the true secret, the grand recipe for felicity. The idle are the only wretched. In a world which furnishes so many employments which are useful, and so many which are amusing, it is our own fault if we ever know what ennui is.

THOMAS JEFFERSON, letter to his daughter, Martha Jefferson, May 21, 1787

Those who retire without some occupation can spend their time only in talking about their ills and pills.

HERBERT HOOVER

Better to remain silent and be thought a fool than to speak out and remove all doubt.

> ABRAHAM LINCOLN

Associate yourself with men of good quality if you esteem your own reputation, for 'tis better to be alone than in bad company.

> GEORGE WASHINGTON, "Rules of Civility," 1747

Forgive your enemies, but never forget their names.

> JOHN F. KENNEDY, quoted in *The Uncommon Wisdom of JFK*, edited by Bill Adler and Tom Folsom

Always vote for a principle, though you vote alone, and you may cherish the sweet reflection that your vote is never lost.

> JOHN QUINCY ADAMS

When you get to the end of your rope, tie a knot and hang on.

FRANKLIN D. ROOSEVELT

It is said an Eastern monarch once charged his wise men to invent him a sentence to be ever in view, and which should be true and appropriate in all times and situations. They presented him the words: "And this, too, shall pass away." How much it expresses! How chastening in the hour of pride! How consoling in the depths of affliction!

ABRAHAM LINCOLN, address before the Wisconsin State Agricultural Society, Milwaukee, Wisconsin, September 30, 1859

About *the* Presidents

★ ★ ★

1. GEORGE WASHINGTON (1732–1799)
Served two terms (1789–1797). Other political offices held: Member of Continental Congress. Military Service: Commander in Chief of 1st Continental Army (1775–1783). Wife: Martha Dandridge Custis. Died: Mount Vernon, Virginia, of pneumonia.

2. JOHN ADAMS (1735–1826)
Served one term (1797–1801). Other political offices held: Member of Continental Congress, Member of Massachusetts State Legislature, U.S. Minister to Britain, Vice President. Military Service: None. Wife: Abigail Smith. Died: Braintree, Massachusetts, of natural causes.

3. THOMAS JEFFERSON (1743–1826)
Served two terms (1801–1809). Other political offices held: Minister to France, Governor of Virginia, Member of the Continental Congress, Secretary of State, Vice President. Military Service: Colonel of County Militia, Virginia. Wife: Martha Wales Skelton. Died: Monticello, near Charlottesville, Virginia, of natural causes.

4. JAMES MADISON (1751–1836)

Served two terms (1809–1817). Other political offices held: Orange County Council of Safety, Virginia Governor's Council, Member of Continental Congress, Secretary of State. Military Service: None. Wife: Dolley Payne Todd. Died: Montpelier, Virginia, of natural causes.

5. JAMES MONROE (1758–1831)

Served two terms (1817 1825). Other political offices held: Member of Continental Congress, U.S. Senator, Minister to France, Governor of Virginia, Minister to England, Secretary of State, Secretary of War. Military Service: Officer in Third Virginia Regiment and Continental Army (1776–1779). Wife: Elizabeth Kortright. Died: New York, New York, of natural causes.

6. JOHN QUINCY ADAMS (1767–1848)

Served one term (1825–1829). Other political offices held: Secretary to the U.S. Minister to Russia, Minister to the Netherlands, Minister to Prussia, U.S. Senator, Minister to Russia, Peace Commissioner at Treaty of

Ghent, Secretary of State, Member of U.S. House of Representatives. Military Service: None. Wife: Louisa Catherine Johnson. Died: Washington, D.C., of a stroke.

7. ANDREW JACKSON (1767–1845)

Served two terms. (1829–1837). Other political offices held: Member of U.S. House of Representatives, U.S. Senator, Tennessee Supreme Court Justice, Governor of the Florida Territory. Military Service: Judge advocate of Davidson County Militia (c. 1791), Major General of Tennessee Militia (1802–1812), Major General of U.S. Army (1814–1821). Wife: Rachel Donelson Robards. Died: Nashville, Tennessee, of natural causes.

8. MARTIN VAN BUREN (1782–1862)

Served one term (1837–1841). Other political offices held: New York State Senator, New York Attorney General, U.S. Senator, Governor of New York, Secretary of State, Minister to England, Vice President. Military Service: None. Wife: Hannah Hoes. Died: Kinderhook, New York, of natural causes.

9. WILLIAM H. HARRISON (1773–1841)

Served one month of his term (1841). Other political offices held: Secretary of Northwest Territory, Territorial Governor of Indiana, Member of U.S. House of Representatives, U.S. Senator, Minister to Colombia. Military Service: U.S. Army (1791–1798); as Governor of Indiana Territory, he led the fight against Indians at Tippecanoe in 1811; commissioned Major General of Kentucky Militia in 1812; U.S. Army (1812–1814), where he rose from Brigadier General to Major General in command of the army of the Northwest. Wife: Anna Tuthill Symmes. Died: Washington, D.C., of pneumonia, thirty-one days after taking office.

10. JOHN TYLER (1790–1862)

Served one term (1841–1845). Other political offices held: Member of Virginia House of Delegates, Member of U.S. House of Representatives, Member of Virginia State Legislature, Governor of Virginia, U.S. Senator, Vice President. Military Service: Captain of Volunteer Company in Richmond, Virginia (1813). Wives: Letitia Christian; Julia Gardiner. Died: Richmond, Virginia, from respiratory illness.

11. JAMES K. POLK (1795–1849)
Served one term (1845–1849). Other political offices held:
Member of Tennessee State Legislature, Member of
U.S. House of Representatives, Speaker of the House,
Governor of Tennessee. Military Service: None. Wife:
Sarah Childress. Died: Nashville, Tennessee, of heart
failure.

12. ZACHARY TAYLOR (1784–1850)
Served part of one term (1849–1850). Other political
offices held: None. Military Service: Volunteer in
Kentucky Militia (1803), rose from First Lieutenant to
Major General in U.S. Army (1808–1848). Wife: Margaret
Mackall Smith. Died: Washington, D.C., from cholera.

13. MILLARD FILLMORE (1800–1874)
Served the remainder of Zachary Taylor's one term
(1850–1853). Other political offices held: Member of
New York State Assembly, Member of U.S. House
of Representatives, Comptroller of New York, Vice
President. Military Service: None. Wife: Abigail Powers.
Died: Buffalo, New York, from a stroke.

14. FRANKLIN PIERCE (1804–1869)

Served one term (1853–1857). Other political offices held: Member of New Hampshire State Legislature, Member of U.S. House of Representatives, U.S. Senator. Military Service: Brigadier General in U.S. Army (1847–1848). Wife: Jane Means Appleton. Died: Concord, New Hampshire, of natural causes.

15. JAMES BUCHANAN (1791–1868)

Served one term (1857–1861). Other political offices held: Member of Pennsylvania House of Representatives, Member of U.S. House of Representatives, Minister to Russia, U.S. Senator, Secretary of State, Minister to England. Military Service: None. Wife: Never married. Died: Wheatland, Pennsylvania, of natural causes.

16. ABRAHAM LINCOLN (1809–1865)

Served one term and part of a second (1861–1865, died in office). Other political offices held: Member of Illinois State Legislature, Member of U.S. House of Representatives. Military Service: Served as Captain in Volunteer Company in Illinois for three months during

Black Hawk War (1832). Wife: Mary Todd Lincoln. Died: Washington, D.C., from a gunshot wound, becoming the first president to die by assassination.

---

17. ANDREW JOHNSON (1808–1875)

Served one term (1865–1869). Other political offices held: Alderman of Greenville, Tennessee, Mayor of Greenville, Tennessee, Member of Tennessee State Legislature, Member of U.S. House of Representatives, Governor of Tennessee, U.S. Senator, Vice President. Military Service: None. Wife: Eliza McCardle. Died: Carter's Station, Tennessee, of a stroke.

---

18. ULYSSES S. GRANT (1822–1885)

Served two terms (1869–1877). Other political offices held: None. Military Service: Commissioned Second Lieutenant in 4th U.S. Infantry (1843), resigned as Captain (1854), rejoined Army in August 1861 as Brigadier General, and later became the General in Chief of Union Armies in March of 1864. Wife: Julia Boggs Dent. Died: Mount McGregor, New York, of throat cancer.

19. RUTHERFORD B. HAYES (1822–1893)

Served one term (1877–1881). Other political offices held:
Member of U.S. House of Representatives, Governor of
Ohio. Military Service: Major in 23rd Ohio Volunteers
in 1861, resigned as Major General in June of 1865. Wife:
Lucy Ware Webb. Died: Fremont, Ohio, of natural
causes.

20. JAMES A. GARFIELD (1831–1881)

Served part of one term (1881, died in office). Other
political offices held: Ohio State Senator, Member of
U.S. House of Representatives, U.S. Senator. Military
Service: Lieutenant Colonel of 42nd Ohio volunteers in
1861, advanced to Brigadier General of Volunteers in 1862,
and Major General of Volunteers in 1863. Wife: Lucretia
Rudolph. Died: Elberon, New Jersey, of blood poisoning
from a gunshot wound, becoming the second president
to be assassinated.

21. CHESTER A. ARTHUR (1829–1886)
Served one term (1881–1885). Other political offices held:
Vice President. Military Service: Inspector General
of New York troops during Civil War, Quartermaster
General for state of New York. Wife: Ellen Lewis
Herndon. Died: New York, New York, of natural causes.

22. & 24. GROVER CLEVELAND (1837–1908)
Served two terms (1885–1889 and 1893–1897). Other
political offices held: Sheriff of Erie County, New York,
Mayor of Buffalo, New York, Governor of New York
Military Service: None. Wife: Frances Folsom. Died:
Princeton, New Jersey, of natural causes.

23. BENJAMIN HARRISON (1833–1901)
Served one term (1889–1893). Other political offices held:
U.S. Senator. Military Service: Colonel in 70th Indiana
Volunteers in 1862, resigned as Brevet Brigadier General
in 1865. Wives: Caroline Lavinia Scott; Mary Scott Lord
Dimmick. Died: Indianapolis, Indiana, of natural causes.

25. WILLIAM MCKINLEY (1843–1901)

Served one term and part of a second (1897–1901, died in office). Other political offices held: Member of U.S. House of Representatives, Governor of Ohio. Military Service: Ohio 23rd Volunteers in 1861, advanced to rank of Major before leaving Army in 1865. Wife: Ida Saxton. Died: Buffalo, New York, from a gunshot wound, becoming the third president to be assassinated.

26. THEODORE ROOSEVELT (1858–1919)

Served two terms (1901–1909). Other political offices held: Member of New York State Assembly, Assistant Secretary of the Navy, Governor of New York, Vice President. Military Service: Lieutenant Colonel, Colonel, 1st U.S. Volunteers Cavalry Regiment (Rough Riders) in 1898. Wives: Alice Hathaway Lee; Edith Kermit Carow. Died: Oyster Bay, New York, of heart failure.

27. WILLIAM H. TAFT (1857–1930)
Served one term (1909–1913). Other political offices held:
Ohio Superior Court Judge, U.S. Solicitor General,
U.S. Circuit Court Judge, Governor of the Philippines,
Secretary of War, Chief Justice of the U.S. Supreme
Court. Military Service: None. Wife: Helen Herron.
Died: Washington, D.C., of a heart ailment.

28. WOODROW WILSON (1856–1924)
Served two terms (1913–1921). Other political positions
held: Governor of New Jersey. Military Service: None.
Wives: Ellen Louise Axson; Edith Bulling Galt. Died:
Washington, D.C., of natural causes.

29. WARREN G. HARDING (1865–1923)
Served part of one term (1921–1923, died in office). Other
political positions held: Ohio State Senator, Lieutenant
Governor of Ohio, U.S. Senator. Military Service: None.
Wife: Florence Kling De Wolfe. Died: San Francisco,
California, of a stroke.

30. CALVIN COOLIDGE (1872–1933)

Completed Harding's term and elected to second (1923–1929). Other political offices held: Northampton City Councilman, City Solicitor, Clerk of Courts, Member of Massachusetts Legislature, Mayor of Northampton, Lieutenant Governor of Massachusetts, Governor of Massachusetts, Vice President. Military Service: None. Wife: Grace Ann Goodhue. Died: Northampton, Massachusetts, of a coronary thrombosis.

31. HERBERT HOOVER (1874–1964)

Served one term (1929–1933). Other political offices held: Secretary of Commerce. Military Service: None. Wife: Lou Henry. Died: New York, New York, of natural causes.

32. FRANKLIN D. ROOSEVELT (1882–1945)

Served three terms and part of a fourth (1933–1945, died in office). Other political offices held: New York State Senator, Assistant Secretary of the Navy, Governor of New York. Military Service: None. Wife: Anna Eleanor Roosevelt. Died: Warm Springs, Georgia, of cerebral hemorrhage.

33. HARRY S. TRUMAN (1884–1972)

Completed FDR's term and elected to second (1945–1953). Other political offices held: Judge, Jackson County, Missouri, U.S. Senator, Vice President. Military Service: Missouri National Guard, Captain in 129th Field Artillery (1918–1919). Wife: Elizabeth "Bess" Virginia Wallace. Died: Kansas City, Missouri, of natural causes.

34. DWIGHT D. EISENHOWER (1890–1969)

Served two terms (1953–1961). Other political offices held: None. Military Service. Second Lieutenant in U.S. Army in 1915, served in U.S., Panama, and Philippines in 1915 to 1942, named Commander of European Theater of Operations in 1942, named Supreme Commander of Allied Expeditionary Force in Western Europe in 1943, promoted to General of the Army in 1944, named Army Chief of Staff in 1945, appointed Supreme Commander of Allied powers in Europe in 1951. Wife: Mary "Mamie" Geneva Doud. Died: Washington, D.C., of heart failure.

35. JOHN F. KENNEDY (1917–1963)

Served part of one term (1961–1963, died in office). Other political offices held: Member of U.S. House of Representatives, U.S. Senator. Military Service: Ensign, Lieutenant, (J.G.), U.S. Naval Reserve, active duty from 1941 to 1945. Wife: Jacqueline Lee Bouvier. Died: Dallas, Texas, from a gunshot wound, becoming the fourth president to be assassinated.

36. LYNDON B. JOHNSON (1908–1973)

Completed Kennedy's term and elected to second (1963–1969). Other political offices held: Congressional Secretary, Member of U.S. House of Representatives, U.S. Senator, Vice President. Military Service: Lieutenant Commander; Commander, U.S. Naval Reserve, active duty 1941 to 1942. Wife: Claudia "Lady Bird" Alta Taylor. Died: Johnson City, Texas, of natural causes.

37. RICHARD M. NIXON (1913–1994)

Served one term and part of a second (1969–1974, resigned while in office). Other political offices held: Attorney for U.S. Office of Emergency Management, Member of U.S. House of Representatives, U.S. Senator, Vice President. Military Service: Lieutenant (J.G.), Lieutenant Commander, U.S. Navy, Commander U.S. Naval Reserve, active duty 1942 to 1946. Wife: Thelma "Patricia" Catherine Ryan. Died: New York, New York, of a stroke.

38. GERALD FORD (1913–2006)

Completed Nixon's term (1974–1977). Other political offices held: Member of U.S. House of Representatives, Vice President. Military Service: Lieutenant Commander, U.S. Navy, active duty 1942 to 1946. Wife: Elizabeth "Betty" Bloomer Warren. Died: Rancho Mirage, California, after several health complications.

39. JIMMY CARTER (b. 1924)

Served one term (1977–1981). Other political offices held: Georgia State Senator, Governor of Georgia. Military Service: Lieutenant Commander, U.S. Navy from 1946 to 1953. Wife: Eleanor Rosalynn Smith.

40. RONALD REAGAN (1911–2004)

Served two terms (1981–1989). Other political offices held: Governor of California. Military Service: Second Lieutenant, U.S. Army Reserve, Captain, USAF, active duty 1942 to 1945. Wives: Jane Wyman; Nancy Davis. Died: Los Angeles, California, from complications of Alzheimer's disease.

41. GEORGE BUSH (b. 1924)

Served one term (1989–1993). Other political offices held: Member of U.S. House of Representatives, Ambassador to the United Nations, Director of the CIA, Vice President. Military Service: Lieutenant (J.G.), U.S. Navy, active duty, 1942 to 1945. Wife: Barbara Pierce.

42. BILL CLINTON (b. 1946)

Served two terms: (1993–2001). Other political offices held: Arkansas Attorney General, Governor of Arkansas. Military Service: None. Wife: Hillary Rodham.

43. GEORGE W. BUSH (b. 1946)

Served two terms (2001–2009). Other political offices held: Governor of Texas. Military Service: Texas Air National Guard. Wife: Laura Welch.

44. BARACK OBAMA (b. 1961)

Other political offices held: Illinois State Senator, U.S. Senator. Military Service: None. Wife: Michelle Robinson.

"*I Am in Here* is at once heartbreaking and powerfully inspirational. Elizabeth and Virginia together find their way down the mystifying corridors of autism and arrive in a place of communication through poignant and memorable poetry. It is a lesson in life, love, determination, and awe." —**Tom Brokaw**, NBC News

"Elizabeth's beautiful poetry clearly shows that even though she is nonverbal, she has a good mind and is able to type independently. Her writings show that some individuals with autism who appear to be low-functioning have real abilities. Both parents and educators should teach independent typing to children with autism who remain nonverbal. Elizabeth's first words when she was able to type were 'Agony. I need to talk.'" —**Temple Grandin**, *New York Times* bestselling author

"*I Am in Here* is simply astonishing! Together mother and daughter walk through the bewildering maze of autism and end up producing a heartrending and wonder-filled story. Get this book." —**Richard J. Foster**, author of *Celebration of Discipline* and *Streams of Living Water*

"Elizabeth's story is one that so many families confront. Many people underestimate the capacity for learning and growing in children with autism. Elizabeth was determined to communicate and express what she held deep inside. And Virginia never lost hope that her daughter would one day find her voice." —**Suzanne Wright**, cofounder of Autism Speaks

"*I Am in Here* is a powerful reminder that we all face battles in life, and together we can triumph. Elizabeth's poignant poetry is a victory over autism. Her story and those of other 'How People' in this book will inspire you to be victorious in your own battle, whatever it may be." —**Robert F. Kennedy Jr.**, environmentalist and founder of Waterkeeper Alliance; author of *Crimes Against Nature* and *Saint Francis of Assisi*

"Elizabeth has such a strong voice even without the ability to speak. She is a true inspiration, and her beautiful poetry allows her to embrace and share her message so people notice her for who she is and not what people expect her to be." —Jenny McCarthy, president of Generation Rescue and *New York Times* bestselling author

"For any parent who has stared into the abyss, this story of a mother's agonizing but uplifting spiritual journey—and an autistic daughter's equally remarkable quest to communicate through poetry—is a must-read." —Robert Faw, PBS correspondent

"'See me. I am in here!' Elizabeth's words give voice to the need we all have to be seen by our quiddities and strengths—not by our label. No label is more blinding than the gaze-averting strangeness of autism's silence. In this book Elizabeth and her mom give us a brilliant look inside a brilliant child whose illuminating story will entertain and inform all of us who seek to grasp the dimensions of human intelligence and perseverance." —Sidney M. Baker, MD, founder of Autism360.org and Defeat Autism Now!

"*I Am in Here* is a wonderful meeting of voices. They are the voices of Elizabeth and her mother, Virginia, voices in poetry and prose, feelings and reality that stand up side by side to move the reader. Elizabeth reminds us of the loneliness that is felt when one is constantly fighting one's own sensory challenges alone. Virginia's concerns remind us of the continuous worry that a parent of an autistic person has to endure. This book is a great eye-opener, helping all of us to realize how autism impacts not only the autistic but also their loved ones." —Soma Mukhopadhyay, international authority on autism communication; founder of Helping Autism through Learning and Outreach; founder of Academy of Excellence for Autism

"Every professional working with people with autism and their families should read this book. Within it, we can find the inspiration to rededicate ourselves to putting forth our utmost effort to

help people with autism access the best of what life has to offer. But it is also a brilliant reminder that through our work, we have the privilege of seeing some of the most profound examples of courage, determination, and the depth of human potential." —Dr. Theodosia Paclawskyj, PhD, BCBA, assistant professor of psychiatry and behavioral sciences, Kennedy Krieger Institute and The Johns Hopkins University School of Medicine

"Stories like Virginia's and Elizabeth's need to be told. They have produced an incredibly poignant and stirring portrait of a mother and daughter battling autism together and achieving something truly beautiful along the way." —Katie Wright, board member of National Autism Association, SafeMinds, and Generation Rescue

"Elizabeth shatters the myth that our children are content in their silence and have little to say. To the contrary, they are bright and articulate but need their parents and providers to find the pathway out of their autism so they can express themselves. The results are worth the Herculean effort. Mainstream medicine tells us to 'face facts,' 'accept the diagnosis,' even 'cut your losses.' Never. Virginia and Elizabeth prove that autism is what a child has, not who she is—and they do so with grace and style." —Kim Stagliano, mother of three girls with autism; author of *All I Can Handle*; managing editor of *Age of Autism*

"We are once again invited to look beneath the surface and beyond the present if we are to encounter the beauty of the person within. . . . We are indeed blessed by hearing through her poetry Elizabeth's beautiful voice that has been hidden within for so long." —Laurence A. Becker, PhD, founder of Creative Learning Environments; producer of the international award-winning documentary film *With Eyes Wide Open*

"God heals in many ways, and *I Am in Here* is an inspiring testimony to just how many ways it can happen. In striking, heartfelt prose that complements her daughter's deeply moving poetry,

Virginia Breen takes us on a beautiful and heartbreaking journey into the healing power of words, the healing power of prayer, and the healing power of a mother's love. Elizabeth's poetry doesn't just give voice to her own struggle—it gives a word of hope to us all. This book is for anyone who refuses to give up, regardless of how or when help might come." —**Rev. William L. Vaswig**, author of *I Prayed, He Answered*

"*I Am in Here* is a window into the soul and mind of autism—and a clear view of the exquisite beauty and power of maternal love. It is both agonizingly painful to read and surprisingly uplifting. It is an ode to courage and perseverance: a reminder that 'failure is not an option' and that we, the parents, will never give up until our children are cured. This book is a work of art." —**Judith Chinitz, MS, MS, CNC**, New Star Nutritional Consulting; author of *We Band of Mothers: Autism, My Son, and the Specific Carbohydrate Diet*

"A beautiful gift of hope for children with autism and their parents. With humble poetry that pierces the heart, Elizabeth creates a bridge from the world of autism to the world that desperately wants to grasp it. The delicate combination of a child's meaningful words with a mother's insightful remarks allows this writing team to accomplish what they set out to do: promote peace and understanding." —**Therese Borchard**, author of *Beyond Blue*

"The story of Elizabeth and Virginia is a story of love and determination. It is also a commentary with universal application. Not only do we readers feel a new compassion for autistic children and their families, but ironically, we discover that our own human struggle to communicate our soul-self compels us to appreciate the joys and pains experienced within autism." —**Dennis Morgan**, philosopher and Virginia's high school English teacher

I Am in Here

I Am in Here

The Journey of a Child with Autism Who
Cannot Speak but Finds Her Voice

Elizabeth M. Bonker &
Virginia G. Breen

Revell

a division of Baker Publishing Group
Grand Rapids, Michigan

© 2011 by Elizabeth M. Bonker and Virginia G. Breen

Published by Revell
a division of Baker Publishing Group
P.O. Box 6287, Grand Rapids, MI 49516-6287
www.revellbooks.com

ISBN 978-0-8007-2071-1

Printed in the United States of America

Library of Congress Cataloging-in-Publication Data is on file at the Library of Congress, Washington, DC.

The internet addresses in this book are accurate at the time of publication. They are provided only as a resource; Baker Publishing Group does not endorse them or vouch for their content or permanence.

The information presented in this book should not be construed as prescribed health-care advice or instruction and is not intended to take the place of consultation with health-care professionals. The authors and publisher shall have neither liability nor responsibility to any person or entity with respect to any loss, damage, or injury caused or alleged to be caused directly or indirectly by the information presented.

Published in association with Creative Trust, Inc., Literary Division, 5141 Virginia Way, Suite 320, Brentwood, TN 37027, www.creativetrust.com.

11 12 13 14 15 16 17   7 6 5 4 3 2 1

In keeping with biblical principles of creation stewardship, Baker Publishing Group advocates the responsible use of our natural resources. As a member of the Green Press Initiative, our company uses recycled paper when possible. The text paper of this book is composed in part of post-consumer waste.

This book is dedicated
to all special children
and their parents.

A portion of the proceeds from this book will be donated to
autism organizations.

Contents

1

Hope

The Quiet Miracle of "How People"

We read to know we are not alone.

C. S. Lewis in William Nicholson's
play *Shadowlands*

A healthy and happy baby

Beauty bursts forth in the most unexpected places. Tiny flowers push their way through cracks in the asphalt of city streets. And often we glide past these quiet miracles without paying them much heed.

But I can't anymore, because I live with one of those miracles: my thirteen-year-old daughter, Elizabeth. She is profoundly affected by autism and cannot speak. Yet she has summoned the courage to remain optimistic. She has shattered the silence of autism and found an escape from its shackles in the beauty of her poetry.

Bright Future

When you see
A tree
Think of me
Growing strong and tall.

When you see
The sun shining brightly
Think of me
Tough and mighty.

When you see
The water on the lake
Think of the future
I plan to make.

Me
Strong
Mighty
Free

Even with all of her challenges, Elizabeth's determination and optimism never cease to amaze me. At each stage of her life, she has defied the labels assigned to her. Although she was diagnosed by the so-called experts as mentally retarded at age two and a half, her intelligence has now been tested in the genius range. Her poetry tells us about the inner world of autism and shines a light on the world around us.

Because of autism, Elizabeth lacks the fine motor skills to write with a pen or pencil. She types out one letter at a time, hunting and pecking with her forefinger. This process is slow and tedious, so beyond her schoolwork, she seeks the efficiency poetry affords. Each of Elizabeth's poems, and the accompanying brief reflections on them, is a treasure for us. They have been virtually our only way of understanding who Elizabeth is, what she believes, what she feels, and what hopes and dreams she has for her life. This is what we share in this book.

When I asked Elizabeth how she wanted to introduce her book, she wrote:

> **I want people to find peace in my book.**
> **I want them to read my prayers with understanding.**
> **Be at peace.**
> **God loves you.**

As usual, her words are better than mine, and for that reason we have put all of Elizabeth's writings in boldface so that you can easily pick them out. The stories in between are written by me, from the perspective of a mom, with lots of help from some dear friends.

The genesis of this book was a group of friends who love books. Every year for the past seventeen years, the whimsically dubbed Select Literate Friends (or SLF for short) stage a virtual gathering of members on paper, which consists of the members' annual letters, copied, bound, and distributed for all the members to read. The irony of SLF is that it is not "select" at all: anyone can join, and many of us are barely "literate." Each person's entry ticket is their list of top ten favorite books. The sharing has now evolved to an annual baring of our collective souls, including painfully honest chronicles of what is happening in our lives.

For the past five years, I have shared with SLF our journey through the daunting maze of autism. Elizabeth's older brother, Charles, also has autism. But in an ironic contrast to Elizabeth's struggle to speak, Charles rarely stops talking. Both children have made great progress over a full range of social, language, and behavioral issues. Both are in mainstream public school with the help of wonderful, dedicated aides. However, the shadow of autism still hangs, in unique ways, over both children, and I cannot and will not rest until they are well.

Each year the response of SLF to each new chapter of our story, and in particular to Elizabeth's poetry, has been overwhelming. To my knowledge, none of these friends has a child with autism, but every one of them knows someone touched by this epidemic. However, I think the response has been about much more than autism. We are all fighting our own battles, and by allowing ourselves to be vulnerable enough to share our struggles, we find hope and gather strength from each other.

Our journey has been full of surprises. Elizabeth's poetry pierces the seemingly impenetrable walls of autism and challenges the stereotypes those walls create. To the observer, she

may appear to be disconnected, somewhere off in her own world, but through her poetry she tells us that she is deeply concerned about the people and natural world around her. Although her face is usually expressionless, her writings reveal a mischievous side and a wry sense of humor. She may display few emotions, but deep currents of compassion, frustration, and joy flow just beneath the surface.

God Is Everywhere

I could not find the sea
So I sat by a tree
To think of all the wonderful things
God has made for me.
The birds of the air
The animals everywhere
Flowers in bloom
My own bedroom
Food on the table
Poetry and fables
Just to name a few.

God is great. He gives us so much. I know all things are gifts from God. I am thankful for all that he has given me.

Elizabeth has become my teacher, and I am learning to think about life, faith, and relationships in a whole new way. I have come to see the world as divided into "Why People" and "How

People." Why People cannot be at peace until they answer the question of why suffering has befallen them. They look backward and ask, "Why me?" How People, on the other hand, ask, "How can I move forward?" Having been dealt their hand in life, their focus shifts to how they can find whatever healing and wholeness is possible.

Our community of How People lifts me up on gloomy days. These courageous How People face their own great challenges with grace and inspire me to carry on. Their determination, like Elizabeth's poetry, reminds me that the light of God's love can brighten even our darkest hours.

The Things I Know for Sure

There is a God.
I am loved.
The sun will shine.
I will survive autism.

I hear a loud "Amen!" from the autism parents of the world. You know deep in your hearts that Elizabeth speaks for your children who can't yet speak for themselves. They want you to remember that they are *in there* and to keep trying to reach them. Have faith. They *are*. You will.

In our How community, this little poem has become a mantra beyond autism. I have shared it with others who have told me they have put it on their refrigerators, substituting their own struggles in place of autism. For some it is "I will survive cancer." For others it is "I will survive depression, an ugly divorce, alcoholism, loneliness, poverty, or unemployment." On any given day, each of us is fighting a battle that none of us was meant to fight alone.

I cannot explain why our children bear the burden of autism. I'm no philosopher or theologian, just one of thousands of guilt-ridden mothers scratching and clawing to get our kids back from the tar grip of autism. This book seeks to look beyond that daily struggle to find joy and meaning in our journey.

You will meet some extraordinary How People in this book. Together we are mounting a quiet revolution of hope. We refuse to let our circumstances dictate our destiny. We see each new day as an opportunity to move our lives forward. We celebrate our victories, big and small. We pray for the strength to continue the battle. The How People in this book show us the way.

Elizabeth is a How Person.

This is her story.

2

Autism

We All Fight a Battle

Be kind, for everyone you meet
is fighting a great battle.

attributed to Philo of Alexandria

Meeting all of my milestones

Me

I sometimes fear
That people cannot understand
That I hear
And I know
That they don't believe I go
To every extreme
To try to express
My need to talk.
If only they could walk
In my shoes
They would share my news:
I am in here
And trying to speak every day
In some kind of way.

(age 9)

I wrote "Me" to let people know that even though I
don't speak, I feel and understand the world around
me. I want to be heard and respected. I want that for
everyone, especially for people like me.

What is your great battle?

Mine is autism. For more than a decade, I have fought a great battle to heal Elizabeth and Charles. Elizabeth lost her ability to speak at fifteen months of age and fell into silence, but I refused to accept that she was lost, because I could sense her keen intelligence, even when she was a toddler. She had communicated with us, using her sparkling eyes and a growing vocabulary, until the day she was given a battery of routine vaccinations. Within a week, her voice was silenced and all the energy and mischief in her eyes drained away.

Elizabeth was officially diagnosed with autism at the Yale University School of Medicine's Child Study Center on May 16, 2000. It's a day I will never forget.

After my husband Ray and I watched our children complete two full days of testing, we sat in the cramped, windowless meeting room as the Yale doctor joined us and said, "I have good news and bad news for you."

We looked at him breathlessly as he continued without emotion, "The bad news is both Elizabeth and Charles have autism. The good news is you live in New Jersey, which has the best autism schools in the country."

We felt as if the building had come crashing down on us. To this day, I still wince when I hear someone say "good news, bad news."

The doctor talked about the need to get the children into an intensive, one-on-one educational program immediately. Every day mattered.

Searching for any other scrap of hope, I asked him what we could do for the children medically. His answer was essentially "nothing."

At that moment I knew virtually nothing about autism, but I could not accept this answer. We would seek medical help.

That night I took Elizabeth in my arms and cried. "Don't worry, sweetheart," I told her. "Everything will be okay."

She looked into my eyes and blinked hers slowly and deliberately, like a stroke victim, to show me that although she could not speak, she understood what I was saying to her.

I stroked her hair softly, saying, "I know you're in there, honey. We'll get you out. I promise you that with all my heart."

Our journey has been long, and at times I have been in despair and wondered whether I could keep my promise to her. That is why her poetry is so precious: it is her glorious, life-affirming victory. She has always been in there.

Autism manifests itself very differently in Charles. It always has. He did not have the sudden regression but developed language very slowly. According to my mother, I didn't speak until I was two and a half. Charles's older sister, Gale, didn't speak until she was two and a half either, so we weren't too worried when he wasn't speaking at that age. But when he wasn't speaking at three, we were concerned and took him to a local developmental pediatrician who declared that he had a "language delay." For us, as with so many other parents, the *A* word was not the first diagnosis but the last of a long, agonizing list. Once Yale gave us the *A* word for both children, the battle was joined.

Every educational and biomedical intervention that we have used with Elizabeth, we have also used with Charles, many times with very different results. That is why this battle can be so maddening for parents. Every child is so different.

Charles is our chatterbox, whereas most of the time Elizabeth appears to be locked in her own silent world. But we have learned through her writing that she misses nothing happening around her. She writes that she is "**in agony**" because of her inability to speak. Often the only way she can cope is by hitting her head repeatedly with her hand in frustration. The force of her frustration is sometimes so powerful that I feel compelled to put my hand on her forehead to cushion the blows. Times like these are when I most share Elizabeth's agony. I thank God that she has found a voice through her poems, such as this one where she projects herself into a beautiful future by dreaming it into being:

Wanderer

I am a dreamer.
That is me.
The south of France
I want to see.
To travel to a distant shore.
There is something more
I want to visit a place where I can
Help people in need
Maybe to feed
Or plant a seed.
These are my dreams.
I want to do this in my lifetime.

> I want to travel and see other lands and people, not only to sightsee but to make a difference. I would like to teach people how to improve their lives, make their space a better place, and be happy and healthy. This is very important to me.

You may wonder how such a young girl with autism and unable to speak found a way to communicate at all, much less with poetry. Seven years ago, in our desperation to connect with Elizabeth, we traveled to Austin, Texas, to see Soma Mukhopadhyay, who had taught her own son, Tito, to "write" by pointing out letters arranged alphabetically on a piece of laminated paper (commonly referred to as a "letterboard"). Tito is now an accomplished author who remains nonverbal and severely affected by autism. We found Soma because she and Tito were featured on the television show *60 Minutes.*

Soma has developed a teaching methodology called the Rapid Prompting Method (RPM), which is being used by hundreds of children and adults with autism. She starts off by assessing the student's primary learning channel (visual, auditory, kinesthetic, or tactile) and proceeds to teach them interesting, age-appropriate lessons. The student first answers her questions by selecting choices and ultimately uses a letterboard to write complete sentences.

For those of us who have been blessed to make this monumental breakthrough, Soma is a hero. In the pantheon of How People, she is at the top.

Over the course of several visits, Soma taught Elizabeth to write single-word answers and then full sentences with a letterboard. Soma has found that most of her students are so bright that they have taught themselves to read, but the simple act of pointing

to each letter, the initiation of creating words, is a monumental challenge for them. That's why a special approach is needed.

When Elizabeth finally learned to compose complete sentences, one of her first was, "**I finally got to talk.**" Such a simple sentence, but for Elizabeth it represented the end of years of tantrum-filled, lonesome isolation. For me, it was an intense moment of both joy and heartbreak. It was like Helen Keller's signing "w-a-t-e-r" for the first time.

Our children are complex and misunderstood. Elizabeth wrote the "Me" poem included at the beginning of this chapter after one particularly frustrating week with a matched set of speech-language pathologists. The first was an expert in apraxia (disorders of motor planning) and the second was an expert in initiation (getting speech started). After hours of evaluation, the apraxia expert said that Elizabeth's main problem was initiation, and, of course, the initiation expert said that the main problem was apraxia.

These experts, and many others before and after them, could not tell us how such an intelligent child could read words and write poetry but not speak. One even suggested in Elizabeth's presence, "Maybe she just doesn't want to talk?" I wanted to scream. The "Me" poem was her response. When I saw those words "**I am in here,**" I cried tears of pain and delight. She was taking a stand for all those afflicted with autism. Years later, Elizabeth wrote a second "Me" poem in which she tries to explain her daily battle:

Me Revisited

I can't sit still.
What's wrong with me?
My body is doing things
I can't explain.
My dignity I am trying to maintain.
People stare at me
When I rock and shake.
I don't know how much
More I can take.
So much to deal with
Going on inside me.
I wish I could get better.
I want to be set free
From my silent cage.

Some of the people at school who do not know me make me feel uncomfortable. They stare at me. I would not rock and shake if I could stop it. It just happens sometimes. I wish they could understand, but mostly I wish I could explain it to them.

Thanks to Soma, Elizabeth now has a voice, but she still cannot speak. She is my beautiful songbird who yearns to sing. She feels alone and misunderstood. In many ways, her journey is not unlike our own. Most of us have, at one time or another, felt isolated and alone.

High school is not easy for most kids. I was no different. In my junior year, my English teacher, Denny, sensed my loneliness

and gave me a copy of *Look Homeward, Angel* by Thomas Wolfe. Lucky for me, Denny is a deeply spiritual man who saw how this book would reach me.

Look Homeward, Angel was life-changing for me. Wolfe's prose, which reads more like poetry, connected with me in a way nothing else had. Wolfe wrote about the tribulations of growing up, of desperately longing to move beyond the feelings of isolation that beset us all. Ironically, it was his own struggle to connect with others that allowed me to connect with him:

> Which of us has known his brother? Which of us has looked into his father's heart? Which of us has not remained forever prison-pent? Which of us is not forever a stranger and alone? . . . Remembering speechlessly we seek the great forgotten language, the lost lane-end into heaven, a stone, a leaf, an unfound door. Where? When? O lost, and by the wind grieved, ghost, come back again.[1]

Elizabeth's autism has been a barrier and a connector as well. In many ways, I am connected with her more deeply because of her autism. What thirteen-year-old goes for walks in the woods with her mom? Elizabeth's poetry, while speaking of her difficulty in connecting, has allowed her to connect with many. She is prison-pent in her silent cage, but she speechlessly opens a heavenly door in the forgotten language of poetry.

Elizabeth's autism has created the kind of connections I yearned for in my school days. Our shared battle has opened my heart to deep connections with other autism parents. I have witnessed the same unspoken bond between cancer survivors. You don't need to say much. You know what the other person is going through. You hug each other and cry. Sometimes, as Elizabeth has taught me, words are not needed.

3

Preschool

Buried Treasures

For where your treasure is,
there your heart will be also.

Luke 12:34

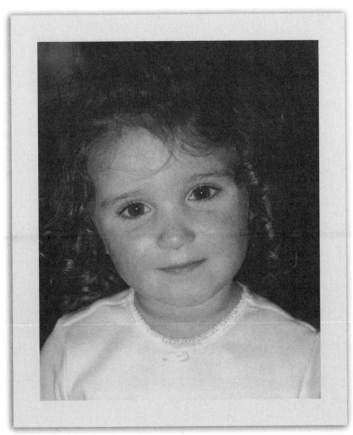

Connected to all before autism

The Bird

Girl in garden counting flowers
In the garden lives a bird.
Children come and go and play
And the bird flies away.

(age 9)

I wrote this because I sometimes feel like the bird. I am overwhelmed at times by the noise and activity around me. So I often feel like I would like to fly or get away from it all.

On one of our first visits to Austin, when Elizabeth was six years old, Soma asked her to write a word that started with *A*, and to our surprise Elizabeth typed, "**Agony.**"

Soma asked her if she knew what agony meant, and she replied, "**Quite so.**"

Soma took a deep breath and asked again what agony meant, and Elizabeth typed, "**Pain.**"

"What causes you agony?" Soma asked.

Elizabeth gave her a sideways glance, filled with exasperation, and typed, "**I can't talk. I am stressed. I have no way to say that I am greatly bored with my day.**"

When Soma tried to commiserate with her by saying she is also often bored, Elizabeth banged her head with her hand and typed, "**But you talk.**"

Elizabeth's struggles to get the world to understand her didn't end when she learned to use the letterboard. Like many parents of special needs children, I set the goal to have her mainstreamed in our local public school. Based on my research, I made the pitch to our school district that early, intensive intervention would get her out of costly special education and mainstreamed by kindergarten or first grade. I asked them, "Would you rather pay a little more now or a lot more for special education until she is twenty-one?" I thank God they saw it my way.

For three years, from the ages of three through five, Elizabeth underwent an intensive program based on the theory of Applied

Behavioral Analysis (ABA) in our home. Therapists paid by our school district implemented the program, teaching Elizabeth basic skills like identifying colors and objects. They taught her in very small increments, with rewards for each accomplishment.

Like most treatments for autism, ABA is controversial. On the one side, there are studies going back thirty-plus years that show a respectable rate of children "recovering," most commonly defined as losing the diagnosis of autism, with early, intensive ABA. On the other side, the critics decry it as inhumane. To them, the process mimics dog training because children are usually given a treat for each successful trial. We ultimately selected ABA because of the concrete results documented in numerous studies showing children mainstreamed in school, even though the process wasn't always pretty.

Our first challenge in putting together our home-based program was getting one of New Jersey's world-renowned ABA providers to come to a rural area to coordinate our program in what they call "outreach services." Frantically, I called the offices of the three Yale-recommended programs virtually every day and pleaded for them to find us a coordinator who would supervise our therapists. Trying to bring some levity to a grave situation, I quipped that we had a special two-for-one deal for them: Elizabeth and her brother, Charles, were both diagnosed with autism. It would be so efficient to coordinate two children under the same roof. Really going out on a limb, I promised to recruit all of the therapists, since they had none where we lived.

When Douglass College (part of Rutgers University) called with the glorious news that they had found a coordinator, I was overjoyed and overwhelmed. I needed to find therapists fast. So I took my cue from Willie Sutton, who responded when asked why he robbed banks, "because that's where the money is." I

started by recruiting the best aides and teachers from our public schools, asking them to extend their days and teach our children after school. One excellent therapist led to another, and we were soon in the business of ABA.

During Elizabeth's preschool years, our house was a three-ring circus of behavioral, speech, and occupational therapists coming and going from eight in the morning to five in the evening. Elizabeth had three two-hour sessions with three different teachers each day. Every night I checked the binders filled with ABA data to see what progress she was making. Once a week the Douglass coordinator came to train the therapists and implement new lessons.

A full book could be written about our three years running an ABA program in our home. We had a dedicated team of therapists, led by Tina, our coordinator, who taught Elizabeth to focus and learn. Mostly, I tried to be head cheerleader, acknowledging and celebrating the lessons Elizabeth had mastered in each of our monthly team meetings over pizza. We've been eternally blessed by all who worked so hard and lovingly on our ABA team. They gave Elizabeth wings to fly.

Fly

I would like to fly
So very high
To be a bird soaring
When the rain is pouring.

I love rain and flying. I wonder how it would be to fly like a bird in the rain. I think it would be amazing.

When Elizabeth was five, we intended to enroll her in mainstream kindergarten, but our school district thought she should be put into its newly created autism class. Unfortunately, the new autism classroom teacher assumed that Elizabeth had acquired no knowledge from her intensive, in-home ABA program. She forced Elizabeth to revert to the earliest "touch your nose" and "look at me" lessons that she had done as a toddler. Elizabeth erupted in fits of anger and rage. This was a dark time.

I could barely keep myself under control at one of our weekly meetings at school: "Don't you think she's trying to tell you something by hitting herself in the face? Don't you think she's telling you that these infantile programs are an insult to her?"

Sadly, there were days when this teacher went further and took Elizabeth's letterboard and communication device away as a punishment for her behavior. When I discovered this, I reported it to the principal, explaining that it was the equivalent of putting duct tape over her mouth. Despite my best efforts, Elizabeth suffered that year, and it pains me now to think that I didn't do more to protect her. (A side note: this teacher left after only one year in our school district, and I've been told that she is no longer in education. Your children are safe.)

I will spare you the details of my struggle to make things right for Elizabeth that school year through my constant calls, emails, and meetings. Only two good things came out of it: one was that her longtime school aide, Terri, shielded her from the worst actions of the misguided teacher and became a trusted second mom. And the other blessing was that in our desperation to prove that Elizabeth was bright and capable, we found Soma.

That year we flew to Austin, Texas, four consecutive months for weeklong intensive "camps" with Soma, and Elizabeth learned how to use the letterboard.

We still visit Soma for intensive workshops to improve Elizabeth's ability to write out what is in her mind. And Terri has remained with Elizabeth, her faithful friend and aide in and out of the classroom. One lesson we've learned: cherish those who best serve the needs of your child. Elizabeth is acutely sensitive to the emotional well-being of those around her, especially Terri, as she reveals in this poem:

For Terri

Feel better, my friend
I am here for you.
Do not be sad
Do not cry
I plan to try
To make you happy.

That tumultuous first year in school included dozens of meetings up the school's chain of command and ultimately appeals to the district's school board. This was a complex matter: I had been an elected member of that school board since before Elizabeth was born. At these tension-filled meetings, I was required to wear two hats, one as a board member and one as a parent, literally changing chairs when I was advocating for Elizabeth.

At the end of that first year, I was not looking forward to facing the seven members of the school's Child Study Team to determine a plan for Elizabeth's next year of education. Elizabeth was now six years old, and the question of whether she was ready to be mainstreamed—put into a regular kindergarten class accompanied by an aide—became more urgent for me with each passing day.

After the awkward pleasantries and formalities, the head of the Child Study Team took an exasperated breath and said, "We are in unanimous agreement that Elizabeth is not ready for kindergarten. She should remain in the autism classroom next year."

Given the report from her teacher specifying that sitting cross-legged was a kindergarten requirement that Elizabeth was sorely missing, I was not surprised by this institutional conclusion.

Slowly, I looked into each of their faces in turn and calmly said, "Yes, you are absolutely right. She's not ready for kindergarten."

Then I drew in a deep breath and said, "She's ready for first grade."

Jaws dropped, but I believed in my daughter and saw the progress she was making in communicating her intelligence and knowledge through her letterboard. I also knew Terri and an exceptional, loving first-grade teacher, Cathy, were both up for the challenge.

The following year, our team of three (parent, teacher, and aide), figured out how to integrate Elizabeth into a mainstream classroom without overwhelming her or disrupting the learning of her classmates. Don't misunderstand: it wasn't easy. Everything we did was scrutinized by the Child Study Team, but in the end we succeeded due to the dedication and perseverance of Elizabeth, Cathy, and Terri. We were on a mission together.

Over the years I've learned there are two types of teachers, perhaps driven by their personality as much as their professional history. One type will generally view special-needs children as problems to be endured. The other will see them as treasures waiting to be unearthed. To those teachers, the How teachers, who see the treasures and have the strength and courage to go digging, we parents are forever in debt.

Hidden Treasures

On another day
Far away
A boat did go
Where tomorrows begin
And days end.
Over the horizon
Stormy skies
A net each
To gather treasure.

I like looking out at the vast horizon of the ocean. It seems endless. I often wish I could go out on a boat and follow it to the end, looking for treasures along the way.

4

Wall Street and Autism

Living in Two Worlds

You have got to keep autistic children engaged with the world. You cannot let them tune out.

Temple Grandin

Mom giving comfort in dark days

Live and Let Live

Am I on display?
Why do they look at me that way?
I want to say
I am okay.
Sometimes I do things you may wonder about.
Just let me be and don't try to figure it out.

(age 9)

I am happy in my body until someone makes me feel different. My gift to doctors would be putting myself at their disposal. They could become better educated and help people with autism.

Most people remember where they were on September 11, 2001. The World Trade Center had been my stomping ground for eight years while I worked on Wall Street. The week before, I was on the thirty-first floor of the South Tower trying to raise money for my next venture capital fund. But on 9/11, I wasn't in New York. I was at home, on the phone with the director of a local nursery school, pleading with her to let Elizabeth into her program.

"She's nonverbal but very bright, and we have a very nice woman, an aide, who will come with her to make sure that everything goes smoothly."

"Excuse me," said the headmistress. "Someone just came into my office and said that there was some kind of emergency at the Twin Towers. Do you think that we should talk later?"

"Can we just finish this up quickly?" I asked. "Can she please, please join the class next week as a trial? I know that you will love her."

I wasn't sure how well my assurance was received because during the call Elizabeth was crying so loudly as to be heard on both ends of the line. Actually, she had cried, screamed, and banged her head on our wood floors for much of the past three years. To top it off, most nights she was awake, laughing maniacally and jumping on her bed. I probably could have better dealt

with the crying during the day if my head wasn't splitting from the sleep deprivation.

This is the story of all autism parents: caught between two worlds, one of which always feels as though it's about to crumble beneath our feet at any moment. Just like the World Trade Center, what you think is indestructible can turn out to be unexpectedly vulnerable under enormous pressure. Life is perpetually unstable and has the potential to take you down a deep, dark hole. I watched my beautiful, healthy child slip away from me into the chaos of autism, and I struggle every day not to be sucked down that hole along with her.

As much as I'm keenly aware of being caught between two worlds, I'm aware that children with autism are caught between two worlds as well. Elizabeth is desperately trying to navigate the shoals of adolescence and make her way through the mainstream school system like any other child. Yet she is also locked into a silent world that isolates her from her peers.

Although my stress and the conflict between my worlds cannot compare to Elizabeth's, I have difficulty finding times and places to rest. My mom has often asked me, "Ginnie, you have so much pressure at home. Why don't you find work that is less stressful?" I have pondered this many times in the past decade, and the best that I can come up with is that somehow the two stresses balance each other. Either that, or I'm a stress junkie.

It is true that raising kids with autism is stressful on a minute-by-minute basis and that running a venture capital fund focusing on cash-starved, early-stage companies often teetering on the edge of bankruptcy is high up on the stress curve as well. Somehow, though, the lessons that I have learned in one part of my life have helped me to carry on in the other.

The intensity and pressure of a Wall Street career have, to some extent, prepared me for the challenges of autism. For the past twenty years I've worked as a venture capitalist and board member of companies large and small. The smaller the company, the wilder the ride. Industry statistics show that two out of ten start-ups succeed, three out of ten have limited success, and half of the companies fail. The same can be said of our autism interventions.

What keeps me going in both my Wall Street and autism worlds? Pressure and hope. The pressure drives my plans and actions. My hope and faith sustain my spirit.

The hope for entrepreneurs is that they will find the magical mix of smarts, luck, and hard work required to build a wildly successful company. The hope for Elizabeth is that she will be healed by God or medical science, or a combination of the two, aided by the force of her strong will. The hope of ultimate success keeps me going in both worlds.

During my years in the venture capital business, I have been invited to speak with groups of entrepreneurs hungry to know how best to raise money for their companies. In order to spice things up a bit, I usually conclude my presentation with "The 24 'Show Me's.'" My mentor in the venture capital business originated the list as "The 12 'Show Me's,'" and over time it has grown. These "Show Me's" are the qualities that an early-stage company needs to demonstrate before I will invest. As I reflect on the "Show Me's," I realize they represent not only a checklist for making investments but also a set of organizing principles for managing the chaos of autism. I'd like to share a few of them with you—let the slideshow begin.

"Show Me" Focus and Flexibility

In both venture capital and autism, the ultimate goals are clear: "going public" for the company and "recovery" for the child. Without losing sight of their ultimate objectives, successful teams stay focused on the day-to-day execution of their detailed plans. The best business plans and medical plans constantly change based on new information. Successful parents and entrepreneurs show the flexibility to employ new tactics and strategies when the current ones are not showing results.

Children with autism have trouble with flexibility, making changes in simple routines traumatic. For example, as a toddler, Elizabeth would get quite upset if we even took a different route to the supermarket. Elizabeth likes routine and dislikes the pressure of being pulled in many directions.

So Much to Do

There was a girl
Who spent her life in a whirl
Going here and there
With no time to spare.
She missed the times
When the bells would chime.
Anxious to fill her day
She did not see the flower blooming
Or the airplane zooming.
She missed some of the best of life
In her strife
To do it all.

> Kids today are kept so busy with activities away from home or at daycare centers. I think spending time with family, nature, and friends is very important. I like to enjoy everything that is happening and not be rushed.

"Show Me" a Committed Team

Battling autism and building companies both require a team effort. No entrepreneur builds a company by himself, and no parent recovers a child alone.

Our first stop in putting together a team to treat the children was the Autism Research Institute (ARI). With the slogan "Autism is treatable," they had the approach I was looking for after Yale's declaration that nothing could be done medically. In those early days of despair, I eagerly read ARI's research showing the effectiveness of special diets and supplements in recovering children. It gave me hope and a place to focus my energies.

Finding an experienced, ARI-trained doctor to guide the children's treatment was the critical first step for recruiting the rest of the team. I wanted a doctor who saw parents as partners. Today our committed team includes doctors, school administrators, teachers, aides, therapists, clergy, family, and friends from across the country. We have seen specialists in New York, New Jersey, Pennsylvania, Texas, California, Arizona, New Mexico, Florida, Washington, Wisconsin, Massachusetts, Maryland, and probably some places I have forgotten. Like companies whose workers are spread across the country, we have a virtually connected team working to heal the children.

A key team member often forgotten is the educational aide. Terri has been by Elizabeth's side since she was three years old.

Most parents are astounded when I tell them this and ask how we have made it work in an educational system that often assigns multiple aides in a single year.

The answer is complex and lies in finding and nurturing a relationship with the right person. We looked for someone who thought being an aide was more than just a job. Terri wanted to make a difference in a child's life. It also required a pragmatic and flexible school administration.

For our part, we try to show Terri our appreciation for her extra efforts. She has come with us to Texas to be trained by Soma. We have helped her find ways to supplement her income. Terri comes to our home every day after school to do homework with Elizabeth and works with her in the summer. She loves Elizabeth and knows that she is making a difference in her life.

We have been blessed to have located two such angels for our children. Just as Terri "fits with" Elizabeth, our son Charles fits with his educational aide, Tammy. Charles's needs are very different from Elizabeth's, and Tammy has been a second mom to him for more than seven years. She knows just when to snap her fingers to get Charles refocused on the teacher. Tammy models the social interactions that are so difficult for him. She comes to our house every day after school to help him organize his homework. Tammy loves Charles and knows that she is making a difference in his life.

Our children are successfully mainstreamed in public school because of the relentless commitment of these two women.

Special Helpers

You are my fortress
In times of trouble,
In times of storms
You are there to guide me.
I hope you will never leave.
What would I do? I can't conceive.
We are a team, the two of us.
You are someone who I really trust.
Thank you for all you do for me.
How grateful I am, I hope you see.
One day I'll care for you
As you have cared for me.
On this you can depend.

Aides help people like me be able to go places we were not able to go before, like public schools.

"Show Me" a Deep Understanding of Customer/Child Needs

A company has a much better chance of my investment fund writing a check if it has some satisfied customers. With a few calls, I can better understand customer needs and learn why they bought the company's product. Was it the cheapest product on the market? The only one that had a certain feature? My most successful companies have been downright obsessed with customer satisfaction.

Autism moms are obsessed with understanding the unique needs of their kids. For years a group of us posted our questions and answers on an invitation-only site aptly called "Dr. Moms." The site was run by the top Dr. Mom, Judy, who works day and night trying to understand the needs of her handsome son, Alex, who is severely affected by autism.

Judy has searched the world for answers to the dietary and immune issues that are common among those diagnosed with autism. After success with Alex, she convinced many of us to try the Specific Carbohydrate Diet. The elimination of refined sugar, grains, and starch helps relieve the painful intestinal distress suffered by many of our kids. It worked well for Elizabeth.

Another common trait associated with autism is an overly active immune system that never shuts down, not even when its job of fighting off a cold or flu is done. It is always hyped up in full fighting mode, so much so that the immune system begins attacking itself, causing inflammation from the intestines to the brain. This constant internal fire is thought by medical experts to cause some of the odd "autistic behaviors."

After studying the research and discussing it with her doctor, Judy decided to try a controversial and counterintuitive therapy of introducing porcine whipworms, a tiny worm commonly found in pigs, into her son's intestine. Before you retch at the thought, hear the science.

For millions of years, humans lived symbiotically with parasites in our intestines. These parasites have been stamped out in most parts of the Western world because, in some circumstances, they cause anemia and protein deficiency. But researchers have now discovered that in areas of Africa and Asia where the worms still live within the population, there are virtually no cases of

asthma, allergies, and other inflammatory disorders. Autism is also unknown there.

Scientists believe these worms help regulate the immune system to protect against these conditions. Leaping forward, some doctors are now researching and treating patients with these "good" parasites for conditions such as Crohn's disease, colitis, multiple sclerosis, asthma, allergies, and—*drum roll, please*—autism.

Relentless Judy found a way to get the pig whipworms from a German company that imported them from Thailand. The worms worked wonders for Alex, but replacing them every two weeks was prohibitively expensive, so Judy struck out to find an affordable alternative. She did additional research and found that hookworms can survive in the human body for decades and produce many of the same benefits.

Unfortunately, hookworms are not available in the United States, but that didn't stop Judy. She flew across the country with her parents, two sons, and family physician and drove in the middle of the night to Tijuana, Mexico, to get these worms for her family. The drug wars were raging, and they heard gunfire in the distance as they tried to find their destination. Just as they were about to turn back for San Diego, Judy saw the hotel's neon sign.

Eight weeks after adding the hookworms, Alex demonstrated his first academic skill ever. Despite the best efforts of a decade of special education, Alex had never been able to identify a shape or a letter. On that beautiful morning, his teacher came downstairs and showed Judy a piece of paper with nouns written in one column and verbs in the other. For the first time, Alex showed the world he could read by correctly sorting words. Two and a half years later, with the hookworms doing their magic, he is

progressing through Hooked on Phonics at the age of seventeen. Alex is doubly hooked.

Lesson 1: It's never too late for our children.

Lesson 2: Educational and medical interventions go hand in hand.

Judy's relentless quest for healing worms qualifies her as a How Person. Through her work as a nutritionist, she looks for innovative ways to help children with autism every day. I know because we email each other ideas, articles, or research papers virtually every day. I think we took off Yom Kippur and Christmas this year.

"Show Me" a Team That Can Perform under Stress

Entrepreneurial management teams and autism moms share a life that has a high level of stress. The key question for making an investment in a company is whether the management team has figured out ways to effectively deal with the pressure and move their companies forward.

I witnessed firsthand the management team at Edison Schools perform with pressures coming from every direction. While I was on the board of directors, the team built the largest independent company managing public schools in the United States, running 120 schools in more than twenty states. In most cases, public school districts contracted with Edison Schools when student performance was at rock bottom. Edison's management team performed well, in terms of student achievement, under tremendous pressure from teachers unions, politicians, and Wall Street.

For many children with autism, stress comes from subtle sensory issues such as sights, sounds, and smells. Years ago,

Elizabeth told us about the stress she felt when she saw certain colors and how she found a way to manage that stress.

> I like basic colors for basic things. When things get clear I must not see a quiet color like brown. I am looking at yellow because I feel clear, but when I get all confused I have to start looking for my DVD. DVDs can have smooth color effects. They are really noisy in a good way. Not at all confusing. But I get so confused when I hear someone ask me something too direct. I like to see bluish colors when I feel relaxed. I don't mind it now, but don't show me brown when I am mad!

To this day, not one piece of clothing in Elizabeth's closet is brown. Why take a chance? This passage helped me understand why she watched so many videos as a youngster. She effectively managed her stress by watching Disney videos whose primary colors soothed her.

"Show Me" Strong Evidence of Pain Relief

A company needs to have a compelling value proposition which remedies a critical pain point for its customers. In other words, the company's product is a must-have solution. When that dynamic exists in a large and growing market, I'm an investor.

For Elizabeth, Soma offered that kind of pain relief when she taught Elizabeth to communicate on the letterboard. It was a must-have solution.

Today Soma continues to offer pain relief to Elizabeth because they have such a special relationship. Soma is probably the closest thing that Elizabeth will ever have to a therapist. I know this because I recently asked Elizabeth if she wanted to go to a local therapist and she typed, **"No, my business is private."** But when Elizabeth "talks" with Soma, nothing is out of bounds. Elizabeth is curious about all the same things that other thirteen-year-olds are curious about, and I have found myself blushing during their sessions.

In a recent visit with Soma, we tried to get a better understanding of how to help Elizabeth when she is in distress. Like most of us, she finds it hard to communicate in the midst of an emotional outburst. Putting a letterboard in front of her when she is upset compounds the problem.

Soma: What can Mom do if you are crying?

Elizabeth: **Always give choices.**

Mom: Let's do that to figure out why you were crying last night.

Soma: Was something hurting on your body? *N* for no and *Y* for yes.

Elizabeth: **N**

Soma: Were you sad?

Elizabeth: **N**

Soma: Were you angry?

Elizabeth: **N**

Soma: Were you overwhelmed?

Elizabeth: **Y. Crying takes much of my energy out.**

Soma: It unplugs your energy?

Elizabeth: Y. I need to clean my mind. My crying has nothing to do with sorrow. It is my energy coming out.

Mom: And why do you bang your head?

Elizabeth: **Body gets hot inside and that way it feels calm later. And I can't live or function in that heat. My body was angry, not my soul.**

Soma: Is there anything that we could do to stop your banging your head?

Elizabeth: **I don't find pain by doing it.**

Soma: But it is difficult for people to watch.

Elizabeth: **I don't want them to watch.**

This discussion has given me some comfort and guidance to better deal with the meltdowns that occur. To know that crying releases energy for Elizabeth and is not usually related to sorrow makes it easier for me to handle. I still have a hard time when she bangs her head, even though she says it doesn't cause her pain.

"Show Me" Fire in the Belly

Entrepreneurs and autism moms are among the most driven, passionate people I have ever met. We have a saying in the venture capital business: a successful entrepreneur must be willing to chew through a wall. I know many autism moms who have done that and more to help their kids.

One entrepreneur I had the honor of working with early in my career came to this country from the Czech Republic with three dollars in his pocket. He quickly got a job at a local supermarket and learned the secret of growing a business with its own working capital. In short, the business collected from its

customers immediately and paid its vendors in thirty days. This entrepreneur bought a small deli and then a bigger store. When I met him, he had a twenty-million-dollar operation. With some venture capital from my firm, he grew the company to a one-billion-dollar enterprise. This man chewed through many walls.

Even this type of relentless dedication, though, can pale in comparison to that of the autism moms who chew through walls called Individualized Education Programs (IEPs) to get the services their children need. IEP meetings are held annually to determine the services necessary for a child with special needs. Although I have never had an unpleasant IEP meeting, many autism moms face daunting bureaucratic hurdles and even need to bring their lawyers with them in order to get appropriate services for their children.

Some of my closest friends are relentless autism moms whom I have never met face-to-face. We have met on the internet, creating our own virtual network of support. I know that I can email them at any hour with some panicked question and they will send it out on our network to get the answer. Mostly, we talk about poop. Healthy poop is a holy grail in autism land. Enough said.

"Show Me" the Courage to Make Hard Decisions

The process of gathering data and making a decision with imperfect information is eerily similar in venture investments and autism treatments. In both cases, I look to balance risk and reward. Just as there is no risk-free investment, there is no risk-free treatment for a child. Almost every drug package insert includes warnings of complications as extreme as deafness, blindness, and death. These complications are extremely rare, but they do happen.

The decision to place a ten-million-dollar bet on a start-up company pales in comparison to making the decision to stick an experimental intravenous needle in Elizabeth's arm.

The autism journey is an emotional roller coaster of hard decisions. We hear about a promising new treatment and have to decide whether it is worth the risk. The data may say that it only helps a small percentage of children, but if it helps Elizabeth, that's all that matters.

After agonizing over a new treatment decision, my hopes soar. Sometimes the hope even reaches my subconscious, and I dream about Elizabeth speaking to me. We do the new treatment and we wait expectantly. Often the results are that nothing seems to happen. We did years of chelation, hyperbaric oxygen treatment, and vision therapy, all with no results.

After the hard decision to start a treatment comes the hard decision about stopping. If we did it for another month, would it help her? With my hopes dashed, I have a good cry, dust myself off, and search for the next promising treatment.

These entries from my journal tell of one roller coaster ride that was particularly painful:

February 2005:

One of our teachers came back from an autism conference excited by a presentation by a PhD who has treated more than 400 children and adults with autism using neurotherapy (NT). Her studies showed results ranging from good to unbelievable.

NT is the process of measuring the frequencies of brainwave activity at particular positions on the head and then training the brain to be in the "right" frequencies.

Using a two-computer setup with electrodes, the children sit in front of a Pac-Man–like game that beeps when the dots are eaten. The dots are only eaten when the brain is in the right frequencies. The child doesn't have to do anything but sit there. The brain likes hearing the beeps and trains itself to be in the middle band.

March 2005:

We made an appointment with the doctor and drove a couple of hours to her office. She observed Charles and Elizabeth for about an hour and said she thinks NT will really help them. She says she is "sure" Elizabeth will be speaking before the end of the year. It made me cry. Elizabeth will speak! She guaranteed it.

April 2005:

Elizabeth and Charles are put on the NT computer program for 30 minutes each day, four times per week. It's a big commitment, but we are excited! The Pac-Man is eating more and more dots each session.

July 2005:

Elizabeth's readings are heading in the right direction, and she seems to be more alert than we have ever seen. No language yet, but I think she is trying to say more sounds.

September 2005:

Is this working at all? Is Elizabeth saying more sounds? Is it only my imagination hoping for it? Why are we still doing this hour after hour? We'll keep plugging away at it, but there is still no language for poor Elizabeth.

November 2005:

The doctor told us that Elizabeth would be speaking by year-end. She was sure of it. Year-end is approaching and Elizabeth still is not speaking.

January 2006:

We persisted with hundreds of these NT sessions, and despite the doctor's guarantee, Elizabeth is not speaking. Why did I believe her? Enough is enough.

Voices

Not a day goes by
That I don't feel the need to cry
And question why
I am trapped in here
Hearing voices all around me
But not be able to break free
And join them

I am frustrated because I can't speak. Why me? I don't get it. Why do people have disabilities?

"Show Me" Skin in the Game

Despite my best efforts to keep my two worlds separate, sometimes they converge. Such was the case with a company called LockStar.

The year was 1999, the height of the internet bubble. Companies defined as three guys and a dog in a garage with a business

plan written on a paper napkin were getting money thrown at them at lofty valuations. With thirty-five employees, LockStar was further along than the napkin stage. In fact, it was well on its way to building an exciting e-commerce security company.

The CEO, Jane, was a smart, energetic Stanford MBA who had been successful with two other start-ups, and we immediately hit it off. Three months after my fund led the first institutional investment round in LockStar, Jane took me aside after a board meeting and handed me an invitation to her wedding with a smile and a wink.

"Ever been to a Jewban wedding?"

"Excuse me?" I asked, confused.

"I'm a Cuban Jew, a Jewban. Let's just say that it will be a lively wedding. Prepare yourself."

It *was* a lively wedding, with lots of good food, music, laughter, and love. But life can sometimes throw some harrowing challenges at us before we even have time to count our blessings. Three short months after the wedding, I got a phone call from the chairman of LockStar's board. Being a cancer survivor himself, he had a hard time getting the words out.

"Jane has cancer."

At thirty-one years old, she had an aggressive form of breast cancer and was in surgery within forty-eight hours. Following the surgery, Jane needed to undergo months of grueling radiation and chemotherapy treatments. Despite our pleadings for her to take a leave from the company, Jane continued to manage it. The company was like a family, and she didn't want to let them down. Jane would come to work with a wool cap covering her bald head, carrying a trash can to meetings just in case she needed to barf. This took "chewing through a wall" to a new level.

In fact, it was a level too far. Both the chairman, Jim, and I grew worried that Jane was literally working herself to death, and we had to do something. After a painful review of all the options, we fired her to save her life. She knew that it was the right thing, and there were tears all around.

As Jane stepped aside, I became acting CEO, not because I was the most qualified but because I had the most "skin"—invested dollars—in the game and I was within driving distance of the headquarters. Jim and I worked closely with the shaken team, and there was more drama than a production of *Les Misérables*. The company earned some lofty accolades, including being named one of the 100 Hot Companies of 1999.

Today, despite physicians' predictions to the contrary, Jane has two beautiful, healthy children. She is a How Person. Her days are spent taking exquisite care of her children and helping others in need, including giving hope to young women who are diagnosed with breast cancer. A glutton for punishment, she is also looking to get back into the entrepreneurial game.

Jane and I have grown close over the years; you could say that we have become soul mates in this crazy thing called life. This is not the typical outcome between a venture capitalist and an entrepreneur. But our unusual journey together broke down the normal barriers: I was there through cancer, and she has been there through autism. We all did our best to make LockStar a success, even though in the end the company did not survive. But Jane did, and my life is infinitely better because of it.

"Show Me" Integrity

In my years of working in venture capital, I've seen both examples of great integrity and the complete lack of it. There was the

honest CEO who told the board that the new product wasn't working and that the business plan would need to be completely rewritten. This admission of a mistake, especially one that could have cost him his job, took guts. The board saw this integrity and stuck by him. On the other hand, there was the CEO who bugged his own conference room and then listened in on the board's confidential executive sessions when it was discussing his performance. After discovering his espionage, the board had no choice but to fire him. The company later needed to post armed guards at the headquarters.

In our autism journey, I see it as a sign of great integrity when a doctor tells us, "I don't know." Elizabeth is on the road to recovery, but the road is long and winding. Unlike with other ailments, the autism road is not paved or well traveled with the proven treatment options clearly marked. Parents are pushing doctors to try new treatments. Someday the science will fully catch up, but those of us who believe that autism is treatable and its impact reversible cannot wait for the seemingly endless traditional double-blind studies to pave the road. We must charge forward with hope.

5

Poetry

On Her Own Terms

You don't have to suffer to be a poet. Adolescence is enough suffering for anyone.

John Ciardi, *Simmons Review* 1962

Typing on my letterboard

Silliness

Over said to Under
I think we have blundered
What happens in the middle
Could put us in a fine fiddle

(age 9)

I was trying to be like Dr. Seuss.

From the ages of seven to thirteen, Elizabeth has written more than one hundred poems in which she tells us about her inner world and her connection with the world around her. Elizabeth is largely self-taught as a poet, and she experiments with different forms of poetry to express herself.

Elizabeth wrote this acrostic poem about the desert:

D ryness, dryness everywhere

E venings always cold and clear

S ounds echo in the night

E very animal comes into sight

R ising moon is in the sky

T he owls come out to fly

This is her first Haiku poem:

Dolphins swimming near
There is nothing to fear here
They are quite friendly

While Elizabeth does her schoolwork on a laptop computer, she writes most of her poetry on the letterboard. She does not initiate communicating with us because, she has told us, it is "**tedious.**" Perhaps this is the reason she communicates her thoughts primarily through poetry.

Why is poetry the perfect medium for Elizabeth to express herself? Despite fancying that I have a muse, I'm not a poet, so I have looked to others for the answer. As it happens, the poet with the best answer lived three doors down from me when I was growing up in Metuchen, New Jersey. I didn't know of his fame at that time, but many years later, after reading his beautiful translation of Dante's *Divine Comedy* in college, I asked if I could meet with him. I still cherish the copy that he autographed for me.

The bibliophiles among you may know that I'm speaking of John Ciardi, a man who loved words so much that he wrote three books of word origins and hosted a program called "A Word in Your Ear" on National Public Radio until his death in 1986.

In his article "How Does a Poem Mean?" Ciardi recognizes that a poem's every word is precious and fraught with meaning. Most of us ask "What does this poem mean?" when a more penetrating way of asking the question is "*How* does this poem mean?" How does it build itself into a form out of images, ideas, rhythms? How do these elements become the meaning? How are they inseparable from the meaning? As Yeats wrote:

> O body swayed to music, O quickening glance,
> How shall I tell the dancer from the dance?

A great poem is inseparable from its own performance of itself. For Yeats, the dance is in the dancer and the dancer is in the

and disabilities. Interestingly, the poem's shape looks like a girl with her arms outstretched.

Help Me

Sad, lonesome, you can't believe.
See inside of me.
My soul is in pain, you see.
Help me to be who I need to be.
Teach me the way to get through each day
And not do the things that will turn people away
From me.

> I sometimes get frustrated and act out before I realize what I have done. I hope to be able to better deal with my emotions so people won't be scared to be my friend or schoolmate.

Each day when Elizabeth comes home from school, Terri and I sit with her at her desk and ask if she would like to write a poem. If the answer is no, we encourage her to think about a couple of topics for the next day. When the spirit moves her, she composes, edits, and memorizes these poems and reflections in their entirety in her head.

Elizabeth writes her poems on a letterboard, where she points out each letter without punctuation, without pauses, and without any further edits. It is a tiresome process, and we must stop numerous times to confirm with her that we have accurately

transcribed her words to paper. She is a tough taskmaster and lets us know if we bungle a single letter.

Elizabeth *is* demanding of us, and she also has an ambitious plan set for her life.

My Plan

Those that know me
Show me
They understand
I have a plan
To make a stand
For people like me.
Someday you will see:
An advocate I'll be!

I want to spend my life helping people. Autism is only one of the things I want to research. I also want to help the homeless, hungry, and sick people. There are people in our own country who need our help.

Romantic poet Percy Bysshe Shelley once wrote that poets are the unacknowledged legislators of the world. I believe he is right. With her poetry, Elizabeth is taking a stand for those who cannot yet speak for themselves. She inspires me with her plan to help all those who are suffering, not just those with autism. Her poetry doesn't merely draw me into deeper contemplation of life's injustices. It calls me to action in overcoming them.

6

Elementary School

Looking for Ability, Not Disability

We know what we are, but know not
what we may become.

William Shakespeare

Finding my way in elementary school

Upset Today

I get so angry and upset
Because my expectations are not met.
I can't think of a better way
To make you see what I want to say.
I am always sorry later, trust me when I say,
I would rather have a nice day.

(age 9)

"Upset Today" was a poem I wrote after I had an extremely bad day. I am not always able to show people how I am feeling. Sometimes I am not feeling well inside, or I have a hard time focusing. Sounds or smells that bother me do not seem to be noticed at all by others. I struggle to fit in, and succeed most days, but like everyone else, I have a bad day once in a while.

In every encounter is an opportunity to find a clue to help solve this autism mystery.

Several years ago I was having lunch with Simon, a friend and former business colleague, and we talked about our kids. He said that his boss had a son named Dillon who sounded a lot like Elizabeth, and he volunteered to make an introduction. Before long I was emailing with Dillon's mother, and we became fast friends. We agreed to have lunch together on my next business trip to San Francisco, and I heard Dillon's story.

Unable to speak, Dillon was considered "low functioning" by his school district. When he was eight, his parents ignored the experts and bought a communication device. The first thing he typed was "Get me out of special ed. I'm not retarded."

I took in her son's first words with both celebration and heartache. He was finally able to show his intelligence, but to think how he suffered in silence all those years. Since that time Dillon has graduated from public high school, and after fifteen years of silence, he is starting to speak.

Elizabeth and Dillon are not alone. Over the years we have met numerous children with autism who are intelligent. In fact, it is my experience that most children with autism are *uniquely* intelligent. If only the world would assume intelligence and look beyond the odd behaviors.

Elizabeth video conferences with a nonverbal girl named Sydney in Southern California. They type back and forth about poetry and nature. Emma is another nonverbal girlfriend Elizabeth met at Soma's camps. Emma has produced a video that begins, "Me and God hoping to beat autism soon. . . . Autism is what I struggle with, but there is so much more to me than that." Mitch is also one of Soma's students, and at twelve years old, he is nonverbal yet gifted at analyzing and managing a stock portfolio.

Soma has worked with hundreds of adults and children with autism and feels strongly that all have the capacity to learn. Her thesis is proven as each person begins to communicate with a letterboard. Soma has taught many of her students to write poetry. This is one of the first poems Elizabeth wrote with Soma, and it remains one of my favorites.

Clowns

Clowns are a peculiar sort.
Oh, to what they won't resort!
To make us laugh is their mission.
What a silly tradition!

I am afraid of clowns. I don't like masks. I can't see the real person. I can tell a lot about a person by their features, if they are kind. I cannot see through a mask or makeup.

Every school day is a new adventure and a mystery to solve with our kids. About midway through first grade, we were frustrated by Elizabeth's performance on the monthly reading tests, as we

knew that they were well within her abilities. During one of the tests, when Elizabeth was only getting about 70 percent correct, there was a loud noise in the classroom that caused a wave of commotion. Her teacher, Cathy, shut off the lights to get the kids' attention and to calm them down. By some stroke of luck or divine intervention, it was a sunny day, and she left the lights off. From that point on, Elizabeth got all the answers correct. When Terri asked her what happened, she typed, *"The lights were making noise and putting a glare on the paper so I couldn't concentrate."*

The next day, the school replaced the light bulbs in her classroom, which reduced the noise, and the teacher kept them off as much as possible for the rest of the school year.

Long Days

Sit, sit, sit.
Listen, listen, listen.
Bit by bit
I start to simmer.
Little by little
Everything gets dimmer.
Then I blow
And no one knows
What led me to this
Unacceptable behavior
But me.
And now you see.

School is often hard and long for me. I just have to let off some steam sometimes.

At the end of first grade, I asked if Elizabeth could be tested for SEEK, the school's gifted program. Given our history with traditional testing, it was painful for me to learn she would be given an IQ test. In May 2000, when Elizabeth was first diagnosed at Yale, they gave her an IQ test without my knowledge. She was two and a half years old and nonverbal. It is hard to imagine that such a test could determine anything.

I didn't have that perspective back then when I read the Yale report and the IQ number 69 screamed from the page, sentencing Elizabeth with the label "mental retardation." I cried and cried over that report.

Now they were going to do another IQ test. What would it say? Did I care? Did the number have any meaning? I had thrown the other number out a long time ago and assumed intelligence. What would happen if it were 69 again?

Don't get me wrong. I know that an IQ score is only one way to measure a person's intelligence and is by no means a measure of a child's worth. Intelligence is only one aspect of who we are, and it's not even close to the most important. On top of that, many people argue that IQ tests are too narrow or inaccurate to begin with. I know that if Elizabeth's IQ were 69, I wouldn't love her any less than if it were 169.

But I also knew the power of perception. I knew all too well what has been termed "the soft bigotry of low expectations." I knew that, fairly or not, the wrong label could severely limit the degree to which the educational system would be willing to invest in Elizabeth.

Most importantly, however, I knew the many challenges Elizabeth was going to face. My greatest worry was that a deeply flawed evaluation process would lead to a wrong diagnosis and set the course of a treatment regimen, both educationally and

medically, that would overlook her greatest strengths and treat a nonexistent condition.

By the end of first grade, when this test was to be administered, Elizabeth was still inconsistent with typing on the letterboard. Some days she typed quite well, and other days her digital choreography didn't seem to make sense. She was dealing with a variety of sensory issues and biomedical interventions which, at times, interfered with her academic performance.

Would they test her on a good day or a bad day? Although I didn't want to put any worth in the number, I was quite apprehensive sending her off to school that morning. I wanted this test to prove wrong both the Yale experts and the Child Study Team.

I didn't say anything about the test to Elizabeth, but I know that she could sense something different that morning. Terri and I had talked about the testing environment over and over again. We needed her to take it in a quiet room that had a window so that we could have the lights off. As always, Terri would sit on her right side. The teacher would stand behind her and on her left so she wouldn't be a visual distraction. We would have two bags of her favorite gluten-free pretzels for her to munch on and a bottle of water. Every detail was reviewed over and over again, as if we were planning a bank heist.

The test was designed so that increasingly difficult questions were asked until ten were answered incorrectly. Each day, Elizabeth would be tested for up to one hour. After the first day, Elizabeth was going strong with no incorrect answers. What a relief. After the second day, she was answering middle school questions and had only one wrong. By the third day, she was into high school questions. They ran out of questions before she got ten wrong.

The SEEK teacher was delighted to tell me that her calculated score was 164—well into the genius range. I cried and cried.

Although I had told myself that this number meant nothing, just like the number 69 had meant nothing, I was elated. Elizabeth had dazzled them with her answers. The SEEK teacher couldn't give me the test, but she shared a few answers after I begged her.

One early question was "Who wrote 'The Star-Spangled Banner'?" to which she correctly replied, "*Francis Scott Key.*" That is something grammar school kids learn, but the follow-up question was obscure: "What was his occupation?" Without missing a beat, Elizabeth typed, "*Lawyer.*"

One question that I still laugh over is, "What is Social Security?" Elizabeth's answer: "*So old people have money.*" How does she know these things? She told us that she is always listening and that she heard a report on Social Security on CNN when we were sitting in an airport on one of our trips to visit Soma.

Elizabeth hears, and apparently reads, a lot of news in our house. Among the first letterboard questions she asked were, **"What is FEMA?"** and **"Who is Hamas?"** Unbeknownst to us, she had been getting her news by reading the CNN ticker on the family room television.

I still get tears in my eyes when I think back to Elizabeth's courageous first-grade teacher, Cathy. She was not deterred by the Child Study Team's recommendation and welcomed the challenge of bringing Elizabeth into her mainstream classroom. She told me that she believed God had sent Elizabeth to her as a blessing. While Elizabeth was Cathy's blessing, Cathy was ours.

One morning when Elizabeth was in second grade, I was helping her brush her teeth when she started to cry. (Because of her weak motor skills, Elizabeth needs assistance to brush her teeth, tie her shoes, button her coat, or write legibly, despite years of occupational therapy.) After school, Terri and I asked her why she was upset in the morning. She wrote, **"I was thinking about**

the people in Iraq. They live in fear of death every day. I want the war to stop and people to get along." Then she wrote this poem:

Peace

If we all try to get along the world would be a happy place.
Everyone could have their space.
War could disappear without a trace.
That is my wish.

I do not believe violence is the answer in any conflict. People are different, but all people want to be treated fairly and shown respect. I believe war could be eliminated if people followed these rules.

In second grade Elizabeth started to blossom using her letterboard. With it she was able to complete all of her school work and Corrie, her extraordinary teacher, took the initiative to use it with her, first with Terri's assistance and then independently. Corrie's efforts to communicate with Elizabeth directly were a key step in getting her integrated into the class. Corrie made sure that she was included in every activity. In the class play, Elizabeth held up her lines as a big sign. Corrie's enthusiasm was infectious, and the children embraced Elizabeth.

During this year I had a breakthrough of my own with Elizabeth: she wrote her first poem with me. Many parents experience frustration in trying to do the letterboard after seeing Soma do it so effortlessly. After school one day, Terri and I asked Elizabeth why she resists doing the letterboard with me. She typed, "**Mom**

is for fun." Although it is hard to persist in the face of such logic, practice and perseverance are keys to success.

I have been able to make breakthroughs with Elizabeth by using fun as bait. Whenever possible, Elizabeth and I take a short retreat. Usually we don't go far, just to a hotel with a pool, so that I can give her a reward for her efforts with me. We work for an hour and then we take a swim in the pool. We work for an hour and then we go for a short hike. These are intense weekends, but they have produced many breakthroughs, including her first successes at writing words on a whiteboard and typing independently on a keyboard.

Elizabeth is strong willed, and we can only push her so far. She let us know this in no uncertain terms in this next poem where she describes her early resistance moving from the letterboard to an electronic keyboard:

Learning a New Device

I will do this when I am good and ready.
Not because you tell me.
So don't try to push this.
I'll just refuse it.
I don't like it, you see.
It's hard for me.
Just let it be.

When learning something new, I have a hard time.
I need time to figure it out in my own way.

To help Elizabeth make progress working on her new device, we needed a big incentive, so I scoured the internet for a deal. A few weeks later, my mom, Elizabeth, and I packed up and went to St. Martin for five days. It was the dead of winter and we thought that the sunshine and French food would do us some good. The island also has a lush butterfly garden where we stayed for hours playing with the butterflies.

B eautiful, flowing

U p, up and away

T wisting

T wirling

E ndless days

R are and lovely

F luttering around

L ike a fairy

Y oung and merry

My magical moment with Elizabeth came when we were working on the little patio adjacent to our hotel room and she wrote this poem for me:

Timeless Waters

On an ocean cay
A nested note to yesterday.
Tea under the stars
Eyes stare everywhere.

I was intrigued by her hauntingly beautiful phrase "a nested note to yesterday." When I asked her what "nested note" meant, she typed, **"Like a nest where a bird puts all its treasures, I have memories stored to remember at another time."**

What joy to finally get her to write a poem for me! We needed to get away from the distractions of everyday life to make this breakthrough.

By third grade Elizabeth was hitting her stride. We made sure that she had a few girls in her class who had a close connection with her from second grade. Her teacher, Jennifer, helped us develop those friendships by carving out ten minutes here and there for Elizabeth to have "conversations" with them.

At this point Elizabeth was using a communication device called an AlphaSmart, which has a keyboard and small display. Her classmates loved typing in questions and having her answer them. We also made sure that Elizabeth had the chance to ask questions of them.

Despite the efforts of her teachers and classmates, Elizabeth's inability to participate in the constant chatter of the classroom magnified the social isolation inherent in autism.

I Am Happy

Can't they see what it's like to be me?
I am fine in this body of mine.
I just can't say what I would like to each day.

I wrote this poem because I am very aware of how
some people stare at me. Some people also talk over
me, about me, and sometimes like I am not there. I
am, even if I cannot say so.

Because Elizabeth excelled in math, Jennifer suggested she
try fourth-grade math while she was still in third grade. To me,
these are the bold moves that make great teachers. None of us
knew how it would work out for Elizabeth, but we were willing to
take a chance and be honest about assessing how our experiment
was working. To our great delight, Elizabeth loved her new math
teacher, Tim, and excelled, doing much of the work in her head.

At the end of third grade Jennifer suggested giving Elizabeth
a reading test. Once again I was nervous about how Elizabeth
would perform. She still had good days and not-so-good days.
Terri and I again went over the testing environment to make it
less likely that some catalyst, invisible to typical children, would
set her off.

The test was administered on a computer, and the questions
got harder with every right answer and easier with every wrong
one. Elizabeth selected her answers on the computer keyboard
completely independently until there were no more questions
left. At the end of the test, she was analyzing passages from *Silas*

Marner and Shakespeare. Her reading level tested equivalent to a senior in high school. We had been reading high school texts to her during the summer, and it was a joy to see that they had made an impact on her.

With these capabilities going into fourth grade, we knew that Elizabeth needed a teacher who would challenge her as well as nurture her. Annie was just such a teacher. She could see Elizabeth's intelligence underneath the unusual behaviors. She didn't mind that Elizabeth was flapping her hands as long as she was learning.

One of the most touching things ever said about Elizabeth came from Annie shortly into our relationship. She said, "I *could* constantly be trying to determine what Elizabeth doesn't know. Instead, I *choose* to explore what she does know." Great teachers believe in their students.

Naturally, Elizabeth wanted to continue her advanced math studies, but in fifth grade it seemed like her luck had run out. Unlike the previous year, she could no longer just go down the hall to take math with kids who were a year older. Fifth-grade math was in another building across the street in our town's middle school. Aligning the schedules just wouldn't work.

Then another solution was sent from heaven. Kerri, Elizabeth's SEEK teacher, volunteered to learn the fifth-grade math curriculum and give up her coveted prep time to teach her. With one-on-one attention, Elizabeth learned at her own pace and developed a deep, trusting relationship with Kerri. Together they completed the entire fifth-grade math curriculum and had time to spare.

These teachers are How People who never stop asking, "How can I make this work for this child?" They exist in every school system, and you can find them by asking around. They stand

out because they see each child as a gift. They are creative and send emails with new ideas. They are nurturing and create an atmosphere of acceptance. We have been blessed to have worked with many of these teaching marvels shoulder-to-shoulder on a daily basis to make mainstream elementary school work for Elizabeth.

7

Community

A Little Help from My Friends

The best portion of a good man's life is his little, nameless, unremembered acts of kindness and of love.

William Wordsworth

With dear friends at my birthday party

Compassion

There are people everywhere.
They could use a prayer.
Today.
Everyone has a need.
Take it to God with speed.

(age 9)

There are many things people have to deal with.
I deal with autism. Some people are sick, lonely,
depressed, homeless, and hungry. Everyone could
use prayer.

When I worked on Wall Street, I commuted through the World Trade Center and often passed a severely disabled man in a wheelchair sitting in front of the South Tower, running his business. He had a large, wooden tray perched in front of him filled with gum, candy, and umbrellas. A white cardboard sign that hung off the front of the tray read, "Don't feel sorry for me. Buy something!"

Rain, shine, and biting cold, Al would be sitting there, often accompanied by his longtime friend and business partner, Junior. I got to know Al and Junior over the years as I bought many Hershey bars and packs of Juicy Fruit gum. On some occasions, if the sun was shining and I wasn't late, I tried to talk a bit with Al, although he had great difficulty speaking. But we kept at it, having ever-longer conversations.

I learned that Al had cerebral palsy and although his body was a gnarled mess, his mind was sharp as a tack. He and Junior had met thirty years earlier on the mean streets of Newark, New Jersey, when fifteen-year-old Junior had tried to steal a candy bar off Al's cart. They now lived together at a local YWCA, where Junior took care of Al's extensive physical needs and Al helped Junior, who was mentally disabled. They were How People for each other.

Here was an elderly, Jewish, ninety-pounds-soaking-wet, handicapped man who somehow found a simple but strong,

young, black man, and they had been taking care of each other for almost three decades. God works in mysterious ways.

Like his sign indicated, Al never felt sorry for himself. He liked to take the bus to Atlantic City and play blackjack. He claimed to have won a lot of money counting cards, and I don't doubt it.

As Al and I became friends, I started to store umbrellas for him in my office. On rainy days, Junior would show up in the forty-second floor lobby of one of Wall Street's storied investment banks, and any of the secretaries would happily bring him a box of his umbrellas if I was unavailable to do it myself.

Al belonged to Jews for Jesus, and his prayer group was often found in front of the New York Stock Exchange. On sunny days I sometimes joined him, eating my lunch as the prayer group sang gospel songs. Sometimes we talked, but many times we just sat together, because speaking took a lot of effort for Al. Sometimes he would have to repeat a sentence two or three times, spelling out difficult words, before I would get it. Then he would laugh uncontrollably when I finally did. Just like Elizabeth, he was in there.

Those days with Al eerily remind me of my struggles to understand Elizabeth. She will try to say something, and I just can't understand it. I will bring out the letterboard, and she will start banging her head out of frustration. That's why we usually just sit together, listening to music, just like with Al.

Shine Bright

If I were a star
I would burn bright
In the night sky
I would be far
That way I could have my own place
In space
Away from other stars
So that I would stand out
And be noticed for who I am
And not what people expect me to be

I sometimes get overlooked or lost in the crowd. I
want people to see and hear me.

During the years that I held umbrellas for Al, another fellow
would sometimes stop and chat with him as well. On the mornings when Al was struggling through a conversation with this
dapper gent using Junior as an interpreter, I would pass by and
get on to my office. One sunny day, I decided to introduce myself.

The fellow, Chuck, had been with a large investment bank
and now ran his own fund with a couple of colleagues a few
blocks away. Al had also gotten Chuck to store his umbrellas.
In fact, Chuck had been warehousing umbrellas longer than I
had and threw Al a birthday party every year. Chuck stood out
in the Wall Street crowd.

In time, Chuck and I were grabbing lunch together to talk about
our friends Al and Junior. Was there anywhere else they could live

other than that spartan YWCA? Did they get the right medical care? Was Al losing all their money on those trips to Atlantic City?

We would scheme about how to bring these topics up with Al, because he was a proud, headstrong man who didn't want anyone telling him what to do.

One of our big victories was getting Al to change his will. In Al's old will, he left all his worldly possessions to Social Security because he said that he had received benefits all those years and if there was any money left after he died, they should have it back. After many talks with him, Chuck and I were able to convince him that Junior needed the money more than the federal government did.

When I was deciding what to do next in my own career, it was natural for me to ask Chuck's advice over one of our lunches. I was deciding between starting my own venture fund and joining a nonprofit firm.

Seven years earlier, I fell into venture capital as a stroke of luck, not realizing how well it fit with my entrepreneurial roots. My parents owned and operated eleven different "mom and pop" businesses over forty years. When I was five years old, I bagged rabbit pellets for five cents a bag in their pet shop, and when I was ten years old I graduated to punching out lottery tickets in their deli.

To my delight, venture capitalists get to invest other people's money in promising companies and work with spirited entrepreneurs to help those companies grow. None of my parents' businesses would have been ambitious enough to take venture capital, but living in an entrepreneurial family gave me the itch to raise my own venture fund.

As we contemplated my next move, Chuck took a bite of his sandwich and said, "It seems obvious to me. People need jobs. Give them a fishing pole, not a basket of fish." And with

a twinkle in his eye, he added, "I would be delighted to be your first investor." I was floored.

That is how it began, and I have been on my own ever since. To this day I credit Al, by way of his linking me with Chuck, with giving me the gift of my own business. This blessing of being an entrepreneur has given me flexibility I never thought I would need. In between all of the conference calls and board meetings, I can take the children to their doctors' appointments and have meetings at school. I have been blessed by my communion and community with others.

For me, community isn't simply a series of quid pro quo transactions in which we receive good things for ourselves in equal measure as a reward for doing good things for others. Rather, when we take the risk of investing in the lives of others, we are engaging in the fundamental act of community building. We sow the seeds of compassion in the soil of our neighbors' lives. When that soil bears fruit, it sustains us all. It is a life-giving cycle of mutual support. Our relationships are like a garden: the more we tend them, the more they grow.

A Bloom

Plant a garden,
Watch it grow.
The more you tend it,
The more you will sow.
People are like that as well.
You have to remember
To treat them well,
And they too will grow
And bloom for you.

> Growth is a part of life: from the tiniest thing to the
> highest mountain.

With my flexible work schedule, I have been able to take Elizabeth to Austin for weeklong camps with Soma to improve her facility with the letterboard. These camps focus on academic lessons, but I always bring a list of questions because I yearn to hear Elizabeth's thoughts. Elizabeth will type out short answers for me, longer ones with Terri, but she saves her deepest thoughts for Soma.

When she was in third grade, Soma asked her, "How is school going for you?" She replied: **"School is not a good place some days. Other days it is fine. I can get so scared when I see other girls talking. I try hard, hard but can't talk. I can't say a thing and sometimes I freeze in front of the letterboard. I don't like being watched. I am most of the time."** These are precious words for me, however difficult they are to hear. They give me a window into her silent world.

Despite these personal challenges, Elizabeth continues to reach out to others through her poetry. *Autism* is derived from a Greek word meaning "self" because autism is associated with the person being self-absorbed. Upon meeting Elizabeth, you could easily interpret her silence and obsession with videos as self-absorption. Her poetry tells us the opposite is true.

Friends

My friends are there for me
Just like it should be.
Having a good time,
Better friends you will not find.
This is very dear to me
Because I feel that I am free
To be the way I want to be
And still be liked, you see.

I finally have friends and I like it. To me a friend is someone who is kind. They accept me as I am and want to be with me anyway. To me, that is someone I can trust and rely on.

Elizabeth has the effect of drawing those around her out of their world of self-sufficiency and into a world of compassion and connectedness. In her poem "Compassion" at the beginning of this chapter, Elizabeth tells us to pray for each other because we are all carrying heavy loads. She looks beyond her own physical and mental burdens of autism and wants us to remember those who are sick, lonely, and hungry. Sometimes when I'm feeling sorry for myself, I remember that Elizabeth doesn't dwell on her problems. She reaches out to others with compassion.

In her poetry, Elizabeth expresses a sense of community and our shared humanity. She needs help with daily tasks such as buttoning her coat and tying her shoes, and she appreciates the help she receives.

Special People

I am so blessed.
Whenever I am stressed
There are people there for me.
I can see
Their love and support
Surround me
And I can face the world
And all that it sends my way.
I need to say "thank you."

Being autistic in a mainstream classroom can be
stressful and frustrating at times. I have been blessed
with people who care about me and help me to work
through my problems. I just want to say "thank you."

When I feel all alone in the battle, I think about the special
people in our lives and, like Elizabeth, I try to "**see their love and
support surround me.**" In addition to family and friends, two
groups have provided great support to me in this autism battle:
my Select Literate Friends and Dr. Moms.

Every year for more than seventeen years running, the face-
tiously named Select Literate Friends (SLF) has come together
as a community on paper. My dear friend and fellow venture
capitalist, Fred, started SLF because he was on the hunt for great
books and asked a few friends to email him a list of their top ten
favorite books. From the 153 of us who participated that first
year, the network effect of each friend telling a few friends who

told a few friends (on top of Fred's tireless recruiting) has created a community. At first we were united by our love of books, but we have now shared all sorts of other silly and serious slices of our lives. You might consider spreading this idea. Ask a few friends to swap their top ten book lists, and it could blossom into an SLF community of your own.

In the beginning of SLF, I followed the suggested topic such as top ten movies or places; then the chaos of autism hit and I just could not find the words. Like Elizabeth, I had no voice of my own to share. So what did I do? I did exactly what Elizabeth did. I found my voice through poetry.

In 1999, I submitted my favorite poem, William Wordsworth's "Ode: Imitations of Immortality." I sent in the whole ode, all 208 lines of it, for my SLFs to bask in its glory. Extracting only a few lines of this masterpiece and having it make sense is a challenge, but I want to share them with you, my new Select Literate Friends.

> There was a time when meadow, grove, and stream,
>   The earth, and every common sight,
>   To me did seem
>   Apparelled in celestial light,
>
> .   .   .   .
>
> The things which I have seen I now can see no more.
>
> .   .   .   .
>
> Whither is fled the visionary gleam?
> Where is it now, the glory and the dream?
>
> .   .   .   .
>
> Our birth is but a sleep and a forgetting:
> The Soul that rises with us, our life's Star,
>   Hath had elsewhere its setting,
>
> .   .   .   .

But trailing clouds of glory do we come
From God, who is our home:

. . . .

We will grieve not, rather find
Strength in what remains behind;

. . . .

Out of human suffering;
In the faith that looks through death,

. . . .

Thanks to the human heart by which we live,
Thanks to its tenderness, its joys, and fears,
To me the meanest flower that blows can give
Thoughts that do often lie too deep for tears.[1]

Wordsworth beautifully captures the arc of human experience as well as his love of nature, God as our home, lost innocence, gained perspective, suffering, kindness, and thanksgiving. In college I studied this poem, but I had a hard time writing the required paper because it was so awe-inspiring. I felt the ode with my heart, not my head.

After years of submitting the writings of others to SLF, I found my voice only after Elizabeth found hers on the letterboard. Mine was a weak, squeaky voice in that first autism journey letter. As Wordsworth ministered in his "Ode," I tried not to grieve but to find strength in what was left behind. We were still suffering, but we had thanks to give, and I gave it in those letters.

After all our SLF submissions are sent in, Fred binds them and sends them to all the participants as a Christmas gift. The SLF entries include contact information so we can communicate with each other between the annual letters. In the years that this group has followed our autism journey, I have received precious emails and phone calls cheering us on. Most ask if they can share

Elizabeth's story and poetry with a friend or family member who has a child with autism.

Fred has often told me how he is tickled by the connections his hobby has created. The year Fred selected the topic of "heroes," he was overwhelmed with stories of adult children finally being able to tell their mom or dad how they felt about them. There were stories about teacher heroes, business heroes, and grandparent heroes as well.

Letter writing has become a lost art, but thanks to Fred's hobby, we all stop for a moment and tell someone how much they mean to us. Years from now, these letters will be our legacy, our love notes to the future.

SLF helped me find my voice and write such a letter to my dad when he became ill. Although my brother, my sister, and I all knew he loved us, Dad had a hard time telling us. Maybe it was his upbringing by alcoholic parents who didn't think boys should show their emotions. Maybe it was three years in the Marines where softness was scorned. For whatever reason, Dad told us he loved us by fixing a toilet or rewiring a light switch, not by uttering the words. As Elizabeth has shown me, some communication goes beyond words.

But I did want my father to hear those words from me before I lost the chance to say them, so with Fred's inspiration, I sat down and wrote him a letter, telling him everything that was on my heart and how grateful I was for the memories that we had shared and the lessons he had taught me. My letter concluded with the words that were so difficult for him to say: I love you.

I carried that letter with me for weeks, looking for the right time to give it to him. My dad rose before dawn to start work each morning, so I knew he was very ill when he could no longer work the register at my parents' antique cooperative. His breathing

had become labored. One quiet evening, I tearfully handed him the letter. After reading it, he had a tear in his eye too.

Elizabeth was only a year old when her Poppie died, but she will have that special letter to remember him.

After almost two decades, the bonds that these SLF letters have created are so strong that Fred now hosts a weekend gathering every other summer at his home in rural Pennsylvania. Many SLFs happen to have staggering musical capabilities, so there is always someone on the makeshift stage singing or playing an instrument or both. The heartiest of the group pitch tents and spend the night down by his frog pond.

What I haven't told you about Fred is that he has had his own share of suffering, and he too is a How Person.

Fred was born with his heart upside down and backward. I know the doctors in the audience are saying, "Yeah, right." But Fred and his cardiologists swear to it, and I have seen the pictures.

A few years back, the good doctors advised Fred to get a defibrillator implanted in his chest. He has done so twice (thanks to a product recall) and lives every day to its fullest. And for Fred, "fullest" doesn't mean European vacations, but it means connecting with people.

Malcolm Gladwell had people like Fred in mind when he defined "Connectors" in his book *The Tipping Point* as "people with a special gift for bringing the world together."[2] Besides gathering SLF submissions annually, Fred sends out numerous newspaper clippings, YouTube video links, photos, and anything else that he thinks will entertain or educate his wide circle of friends.

Fred was the first friend I called when I got the news about the children having autism. Knowing he has a special-needs child himself, I had to hear his "How" voice telling me that one could

survive such a blow. He was there for me in my initial terror. Every time a shell-shocked mom with a newly diagnosed child calls or emails me, I remember Fred's calm, reassuring voice, and I try to give them hope. I send them one of Elizabeth's poems and tell them to remember that their child is in there.

Children with autism need for us to keep trying to connect with them. Sometimes these connections are highly unusual: a touch of the hand, a walk without words, watching videos together. Unusual connections—that brings me back to Al and Junior.

After our dear friend Junior passed away from tuberculosis, Al moved into a nursing home. I visited him as often as I could, but autism's turmoil was already upon us. On particularly ambitious days, I brought the children with me. Al shared a special kinship with Elizabeth. Without words, they were at peace with each other.

My last visit with Al was not easy. He could not move any part of his body. I just held his clenched hand in silence. He knew I was there.

A week later, his brother called to say that he had passed on. After a life filled with both struggle and joy, Al was with God. I can see him there, in a glorious new body, without the wheelchair, without his tortured body. He speaks perfectly clearly. That is the way God has always seen him and heard him. That is the way that God sees and hears Elizabeth: fearfully and wonderfully made.

8

Nature

Listening to Trees in Harvard Yard

The most beautiful thing that we can experience is the
mysterious. . . . Look deep into nature, and then you
will understand everything better.

Albert Einstein

With Gale and Charles near Yellowstone

Currents

Oh mighty ocean!
Always in motion.
Nothing can compare
To something so rare.
Maybe I will find a shell.
What stories it could tell.

(age 8)

To me the ocean is a mysterious place. The ocean is calming and exciting all in one. As I look into the horizon, I feel like I am looking into the future which is limitless. The ocean is a place to relax, think, and reflect.

Ever since I was a little girl, I have been amazed by—or, perhaps more accurately, obsessed with—the story of Helen Keller. So when I was a junior at Harvard, a one-sentence advertisement in the student newspaper seemed to be calling out to me: "Volunteer readers for the blind." I dialed the number.

"Hi! I understand that you are looking for volunteer readers?"

"Yes, we are. Do you happen to know Greek?"

"No, sorry, I only know a little Spanish," I replied, a bit disappointed that my calling was so short-lived.

"Oh, no. I didn't mean *Greek*, Greek. I meant all those letters in physics equations. We have a freshman physics major who needs a reader."

"Hey, that's a different story! I've taken enough physics to read equations."

And that began my love affair with Peter, a brilliant blind student. It wasn't an affair in the modern sense of the word but a passionate, innocent attachment which, unfortunately, was only brief.

As a freshman, Peter lived in "The Yard," the bucolic central green on campus, and I, as an upperclassman, lived in a "House" near the Charles River. Soon after meeting Peter, I started bumping into him fairly frequently, often sneaking up behind him and taking his arm in mine. Peter would say, "Boy, it's funny how we run into each other so much." He didn't know that I always looked for the movement of his walking stick tap, tap, tapping

back and forth as he was coming and going to classes. In my daily grind studying computer science and working three jobs, Peter's sunny countenance was a refuge.

Several times each week we would get together so that I could read whatever the university was not able to get in Braille. There were a lot of Greek symbols in his physics assignments, and he would often catch my mistake in the midst of some lengthy problem where I got lost. "Didn't you mean gamma, not alpha?" he would query, and we would both laugh. He could hear better than I could see.

In many ways, Elizabeth reminds me of Peter—each is smarter than I am, and each senses the world differently, almost with a sixth sense. And even more, each of them love music, walks in the rain, and flying down a path on the back of a tandem bike or a horse.

Running Free

Halt, trot, run, to name a few
Of all the things I like to do
Riding has to top the list
Sitting up high I can't resist
Enjoying the outside world
Seeing things from atop a beautiful creature.

I like riding horses. They are very sensitive animals. They seem to know how you feel. I was very lucky to have a nice horse because I jumped off it and it didn't kick me.

As the months rolled on, Peter told me how he lost his eyesight to a rare cancer when he was a toddler. He told me the story with no self-pity or anger. He had developed his other senses to make up for it. He had perfect pitch and was a member of the highly selective Harvard Glee Club. Peter reminded me of Helen Keller, who was known to "listen" to trees.

Helen Keller's story means more to me now than ever. Her mother, Kate Adams Keller, is a model of relentless parenting. Family members urged her to put Helen in an asylum, but she refused. This was in the 1880s, so she had no internet support groups to lean on. Mrs. Keller traveled around the country searching for a way into her daughter's world. From her home in Tuscumbia, Alabama, she managed to get the attention of the esteemed Dr. Alexander Graham Bell, the inventor of the telephone and a former teacher of the deaf.

After warmly receiving Helen, Dr. Bell suggested that Mrs. Keller write to the Perkins Institution for the Blind in Massachusetts. It was at Perkins that Helen met Anne Sullivan, who became her teacher for life. Helen later wrote, "The most important day I remember in all my life is the one on which my Teacher, Anne Mansfield Sullivan, came to me."

Now, some say that these kinds of connections are just luck. I don't believe that. I believe that when we are relentless parents, with open hearts, providential connections happen for our children. Elizabeth's longtime aide, Terri, is to Elizabeth what Anne was to Helen.

To get back to Helen and listening to trees: Dr. Bell also became Helen's lifelong friend. They would go for walks in the woods, and Helen would listen to the trees with her senses of smell and touch. Dr. Bell was adept at finger spelling, so he and Helen could chat during their long walks.

Both Helen and my friend Peter were How People, and they both loved nature. In her book *The World I Live In*, Helen wrote, "The infinite wonders of the universe are revealed to us in exact measure as we are capable of receiving them. The keenness of our vision depends not on how much we can see, but on how much we feel. Nor yet does mere knowledge create beauty. Nature sings her most exquisite songs to those who love her."[1]

Whales

Listen to the whale song
Because it doesn't last long.
Beautiful but sad too,
Your emotions know what to do.
Should I cry? Should I smile?
I'll just have to think on that awhile.

Animals are amazing to watch. A favorite of mine are dolphins. I find that they and whales are very intelligent. The noises they make to communicate are fascinating and a little sad at the same time.

In the middle of my friend Peter's sophomore year, the cancer that took his eyesight returned. After numerous surgeries and treatments, Peter said that he'd had enough and that he was at peace with letting nature take its course. Peter was supposed to play the organ at my wedding but died three days before the event. As I held his corsage in my hand, I knew he was there in spirit.

Peter's life was so brief, but it had such an impact on me. I wanted to make sure I honored his memory by continuing to read for the blind. After moving back to my hometown after graduation, I called our county office for social services. They told me a blind, single mother had been persistently calling them for a reader. Little did I know how much this young mother would teach me about being relentless.

With a name and address in hand, I drove a couple of towns over to meet Kathy and her two small children. Kathy's piled-up mail was waiting for me. We quickly got into a rhythm of knowing what needed to be read and filled out or filed and what could be thrown away. I balanced her checkbook, and we agreed to meet the following week.

Week after week, month after month, we read mail and did paperwork, and our friendship grew. I learned that Kathy is a fighter in the best sense of the word. Despite her own health problems, she fought to get the right medical care for her children. She fought to keep her house when her divorce got ugly. She fought to earn a two-year college degree. She fought for special educational services for her kids. I helped as much as I could with each of these battles, learning from her determination with each step.

Kathy is a How Person.

Twenty-five years later, I still read for Kathy and still stay in touch with Peter's mother, Betty.

Kathy has recently been diagnosed with cancer and is fighting it with her usual grace and determination. She doesn't complain about the chemotherapy. She just wants to be there when her daughter graduates from college in the spring.

Over the years I have sent Elizabeth's poems to Betty, and I hope in some small way they have brought her some comfort

and joy. Betty is a gardener and has always enjoyed Elizabeth's nature poems. Peter was her only child, and she loved him in a way I can now only begin to understand. When Peter was with us, he soared, and today he has wings.

Wings

On a sunny day
The birds play
Kites fly
In the sky.
Why can't I?

I want to fly. I want wings. I want to soar high, go places.

In his book *Nature*, Ralph Waldo Emerson wrote: "To speak truly, few adult persons can see nature. Most persons do not see the sun. At least they have a very superficial seeing. The sun illuminates only the eye of the man, but shines into the eye and the heart of the child."[2] Such a child was Peter, and so too is Elizabeth.

Colorful World

If I were a flower which one would I be?
There are so many choices, you see.
Maybe a sunflower
As high as a tower.
I might be a rose
With a regal pose.
What about a daisy?
Is that too crazy?
I think I would be a lily
Pretty and frilly.

Nature reminds me of people. Mimi is a sunflower,
tall and bright. Terri is a rose, small and special. My
mom is a daisy, beautiful and fun. I am a lily, pretty,
frilly, and silly.

I've often wondered why nature is so important to Elizabeth, even more so than to most children. I've come to believe it's because nature provides an antidote to the sensory overload that is so prevalent in our culture and so difficult for children with autism. Under the best of circumstances, Elizabeth experiences the world in a way that can be simply overwhelming. Sights, sounds, smells, colors—she experiences all of these to an unusually intense degree. For those of us whose senses have become hardened to the blaring cacophony of the modern world, with its steady diet of car horns, neon lights, television commercials, and near-constant background music, it's difficult to

train ourselves to understand how overwhelming our world truly is for those with autism.

Chicago

The city is a crowded place
With things crammed into a small space.
Activity here and there.
Sometimes I think it's just not fair
To expect me to take it all in.

Chicago is a big city. It is full of things to see and hear. I often become overcome in this kind of place. It is exciting and exhausting at the same time.

I believe Peter would have understood Elizabeth. As a result of his blindness, Peter's other senses were acute and highly attuned to the world around him. I know his love of nature was due at least in part to the respite it provided from the sensory overload of life in bustling Cambridge. Although nature is scarcely silent, its sounds and rhythms are much more closely aligned with the natural rhythms of our bodies. When Elizabeth is besieged by the noise of the world around her, we often retreat to the woods surrounding our home, where we take long walks that seem to calm her spirit.

Our favorite walks are in the rain. The rain's gentle footfall on the trees provides a steady patter while the birds and crickets serenade us with their glorious melodies. I believe this is God's design. It's a reminder that we haven't been haphazardly discarded in this world, left on our own to fend for ourselves. We

are not alone. We have not been forgotten. We are surrounded and sustained by a love incomprehensible in its magnitude yet so simple a child can glimpse its wonder in the tiniest raindrop. The poet William Wordsworth understood this well when he said the smallest flower could bring for him thoughts that lie too deep for tears. Elizabeth understands too.

Rain

Oh my, how the rain comes down.
Pounding, pounding to the ground.
Some of you might frown
But to me it is profound.

Weather-wise, rain is my favorite type. The flowers seem to sigh with relief. Everything sparkles and shines. The rain lightly touches and tickles my skin. I like nature. It makes me realize that the world is beautiful. I forget my autism.

Of the many lessons I've learned from Elizabeth, this is one of the most powerful: the world is indeed beautiful. But it's more than beautiful. It's a love note from God. When conference calls, doctors' appointments, and meetings with school officials threaten to pull me under, I am drawn to the steady call of nature, which takes me back to the Source of all that sustains me and lets me know that the rain falling in my life now will bring forth flowers in this world and the world to come.

"Deep calls to deep," as the psalmist once said.

9

Hopes and Dreams

Relentless Parenting

We must accept finite disappointment, but never lose infinite hope.

Martin Luther King Jr.

On a working retreat with Mom

Hard Things

When I am alone
I often wonder about my life
And the things I plan to do.
I know that there will be strife
And sacrifice
But all things worthwhile
Come with a price
If you want to accomplish your dreams.

(age 10)

I have plans to feed the hungry, fight for world peace,
and travel. These are hard goals for anyone. I know
I will have to work extra hard to accomplish these
dreams.

On rare occasions, a movie captures a truth and brings you to your knees. That was what it felt like for me when I watched the HBO film *Temple Grandin*.

Temple is well known for her accomplishments, despite being deeply affected by autism. She has a doctorate in animal science and is credited with designing more than half of the commercial animal handling facilities in North America. Her life's work has had a major impact on treating animals more humanely.

In one of the movie's more powerful scenes, Temple's mother, Eustacia Cutler, opens her heart to the science teacher who will later become Temple's mentor:

Eustacia Cutler: You can't even begin to imagine the chaos, the upheavals, the tantrums. And the pain, *her* pain.

Mr. Carlock: You seem to be acting as if you have done something wrong when it's obvious that you've done everything right. I think she's terrific. I know it's difficult when as parents we want our children to be everything that we hoped for them to be. And if they're not, we think that it's our fault and that there's never ever anyone out there that understands what we're going through, and it makes you feel alone.[1]

This short movie clip says so much about what it means to be a relentless parent—and I choose the word *relentless* pointedly. All good parents are persistent. Persistent parents are firm and committed and in control. For autism parents, we can't settle for mere persistence. Relentless parenting can make us feel out of control, but perhaps that's the point. Relentless parenting is not about being in control; it's about being driven by a love beyond our control. It compels us to act in ways that wouldn't survive a coolheaded cost-benefit analysis.

There is a saying, "We don't choose our children and they don't choose us." That is true for most of us but not true for a woman named Norma Claypool, who caught my eye on the cover of *Parade* magazine on December 25, 1988. Over twenty-one years, Norma had adopted ten children as a single mom. Norma's adopted babies were special children. They all had severe disabilities and, but for Norma, would have been institutionalized. The article spoke about Richard, age ten, who was blind and had undergone nineteen facial operations, and Gayle, age two, who was born with only part of her brain. The cover proclaimed Norma's words: "Most people adopt children with their eyes. I adopt them with my heart."

Norma adopts them with her heart because she is *blind*. It took my breath away.

When Norma was two years old, her eyes were removed to treat a malignant brain tumor. "My mother, a 4-foot-9 ball of fire, would never let me feel sorry for myself or accept any limitations," Norma recalled. "She constantly drilled into my noggin: You can do anything you want."[2]

This woman's courage and commitment blew me away. I had just lost Peter a couple of months earlier, and I felt compelled

to find her. Little did I know then what a special inspiration she would become to me now.

After several calls to *Parade* magazine (there was no internet back then), I learned that she lived in Maryland. Eventually I found her phone number and gave her a call. She talked about her children with great affection.

We have talked every year since then, and I send her a Christmas card with a little something for the children. She now lives in Pittsburgh, and I have vowed that someday soon, we will finally meet. She still has a lot to teach me about relentless parenting. She can teach me how to respond to the tough questions Elizabeth asks me.

Amazing Bodies

The body is a wondrous thing
The beat of the heart
The work of the brain
All the while it works and works
From the beginning of life
To the endless day-to-day strife
It carries us through this journey that's life

Most people have awesome bodies. Why do I have this one? People think I am a freak. Maybe I am.

In my quest to be a relentless parent, I've discovered a number of "rules" that I rely on to keep moving forward. These may not work for you. We all have to march to the beat of our own drum. These rules are my drumbeat when I am in the heat of the battle.

124

Rule #1: Survive

In her memoir *A Thorn in My Pocket*, Eustacia Cutler, Temple Grandin's mother, makes an observation that echoes in my ears: "The first truth, I'd stumbled on, all those years ago: if I didn't survive, Temple wouldn't survive."[3] My mother said the same thing to me when I was wallowing in the depths of despair. My Marine father put it another way: "Buck up!"

Recently, I inexplicably herniated two disks in my upper back. The only pain I can compare this to is the pain of childbirth. I think being forced to remain flat on my back for a month was God's way of telling me to slow down before I killed myself.

Mom's Pain

God, help my mother
She is more dear to me than any other.
She is in such pain
I know that it is hard for her to refrain
From doing for us
Like she usually does.
Let her know we are all OK
And make her better.

My Mom hurt her back. I wanted her not to worry about me.

Rule #2: Never Give Up Hope

Perhaps today's best known autism mom is Jenny McCarthy. In her memoir *Louder Than Words: A Mother's Journey in Healing Autism*, she tells the story of recovering her son, Evan. Jenny worked hard for a relatively short period of time to heal her son—years versus the decades of struggle for some parents. She is wise to recognize her good fortune at the end of her book:

> Not all children with autism will be able to make leaps like Evan. Some parents have worked longer and harder than I have, and with no success, trying the same things. I have no idea why some treatments work on some kids and not on others. But I beg moms *and dads* to at least try.[4]

For more than a decade we have fought the autism fight. After hundreds of interventions, Elizabeth has shattered the silence of autism, but she still cannot speak. Relentless autism parents live by Winston Churchill's creed: "Never, never, never, never give up."

Rule #3: Keep Fighting

Our children need us to be their advocates. The educational side of the equation is just as important as the medical side for a child's recovery. The school system may not think your child is ready for mainstreaming, but you are the one who knows what is best for your child. With a team approach, most obstacles can be overcome.

Elizabeth shares her fighting spirit with another man who believed in overcoming obstacles:

Fight for Life

Fight for life
Fight for freedom
Martin Luther King
I would sure like to meet him
I fight for acceptance
Every day of my life
In this, we are alike

Mr. King was brave and determined. Blacks were not allowed to do certain things because of their color. Autism keeps me from doing things as well.

Rule #4: Look for Ability, Not Disability

Temple Grandin relentlessly pushes for society to find the special capabilities that come with autism. She summed it up with her characteristically humorous candor in a *Wall Street Journal* interview entitled "Life Among the 'Yakkity Yaks.'"

"Who do you think made the first stone spear?" asks Temple Grandin. "That wasn't the yakkity yaks sitting around the campfire. It was some Aspberger sitting in the back of the cave figuring out how to chip rocks into spearheads."[5]

Our children have strengths, and we need to encourage and develop them. Even their obsessions can be channeled into career objectives. If a child is good at systemizing, maybe he or she could be an engineer or librarian or lab technician. Our job is to remove as many obstacles as possible, both medically and educationally, so that they may be productive members of society.

As you can see from this poem, Elizabeth may well end up as an environmental scientist:

You Pollute—Stop It!

What's going on in the ocean
Causing so much commotion?
There is something dirty here,
Something we should fear.
Come right away and save the day,
Or we won't be able to swim and play
Like we all want to do.
Will you?

I get very upset when I see humans act carelessly toward nature. People don't always stop to think about how their actions can kill innocent animals and destroy natural resources.

Or perhaps a meteorologist:

Thunderstorms

An electrical show
Sets the sky aglow.
The pop of thunder
The crackling of a strike
Lights up the night
And gives me a thrill
Like nothing else will.

I felt elated when I wrote this poem. I get very excited over weather. It changes so fast and is often unpredictable. I feel the charge in the air and inside my body. It is an amazing feeling.

Whether it means trips to the beach or walks in the rain, we try to respect and encourage Elizabeth's interests.

Rule #5: Move beyond the Guilt—It's Not Productive

Most autism moms have the guilt gene. Something went terribly wrong with our children. Was it something we did or didn't do that caused it? We are bound and determined that nothing else harms them. I do worry about Elizabeth hurting herself because she, like many children with autism, doesn't seem to have a fear gene.

For me, the guilt goes deeper. I held Elizabeth down for her battery of vaccinations at fifteen months, and I witnessed autism take hold of her within a week. I believe it was more than a coincidence that Elizabeth immediately lost all language and began rocking back and forth, staring into another world.

I am not anti-vaccine. But I believe children receive too many, too soon, and all of them need to be cleansed of questionable ingredients. And for families like mine, with a history of autoimmune dysfunction, the vaccination schedule should be reviewed very carefully. Parents can and should educate themselves to make informed, appropriate choices for their children.

My rational side knows that my guilt is unwarranted and destructive. Twelve years ago, virtually no research had been done

on the subject, and even today, the medical community cannot say for sure if some vaccines cause autism in some children.

While my head knows all of this inside and out, my heart can be a slow learner at times. I hope to rid myself of this guilt someday, but that day hasn't arrived yet.

Until it does, one of the great gifts that Elizabeth brings to my life is her compassion. I know she senses the heavy burden of my worry for her, and I believe she is trying, in her own mischievous way, to relieve me of this burden. This exchange shows the rare blend of genuine empathy and wry wit that makes her such a blessing in my life:

Elizabeth: **Most people worry. Mom, you get too worried. You need to relax because I get so anxious.**

Mom: I get worried when you climb on the fence on Mimi's [her grandmother's second story] porch . . .

Elizabeth: **Did I ever fall?**

Rule #6: Love Is Never Wasted

Loving someone is easy when you feel them loving you back. What happens when that love is trapped behind a wall? What happens when you feel that you are pouring your love into a black hole where no light shines out?

Every day I grab whatever half-hugs Elizabeth will permit. I want her to feel my love and to find the ways in which she can accept it. For now, that way is primarily the words that I say to her. I tell her that I believe in her. I tell her that she is smart and

wonderful and beautiful. She needs to hear these things even though it seems as if she is not listening. She is listening.

Sometimes it feels like the line in *King Lear*:

> How sharper than a serpent's tooth it is
> To have a thankless child! Away, away!

But these are not thankless children; they simply can't express themselves to us in the ways we are accustomed.

It was a great blessing to me when Elizabeth wrote this poem for Mother's Day. I consider it an anthem for all autism moms:

Mom

Love like no other,
Unconditional because
It comes naturally.
Always there,
Nothing compares
To the bond that
A mother and child share.

This is a special relationship. Only one person loves you so deeply and unconditionally. I can always count on my mother to support me and help me to be all I can be.

Rule #7: Keep Their Dreams Alive

In her poetry Elizabeth tells us her dreams of changing the world despite the challenges she faces. In "Hard Things" at the beginning of this chapter, she tells us that **"all things worthwhile come with a price."** She needs me to be a relentless advocate for her, especially in school, so that she can accomplish those dreams.

Over the years Elizabeth has told us that she wants to be president, a doctor to cure autism, and, more recently, a nun. She has big dreams, and I believe that she will make a difference in the world. In this poem she tells us that life is not always predictable, so we need to follow our dreams today:

Happiness

Why do people say someday?
Why not today?
If you always say someday,
You may never get to do things that make you
happy.
So go out and be happy.
Make it snappy!

I truly believe people should follow their dreams. If you always put off things you want to do, they may never happen. Life is not always predictable. If you have a chance to do that which makes you happy, do it.

Rule #8: Be Upbeat

When things aren't going so well at school, I try to be a cheerleader for the teachers who are trying their best. We may not have all the answers right now, but we will figure things out together.

On our long drives to medical appointments, Elizabeth and I try to keep our spirits up by singing songs and dancing in our seats. Elizabeth doesn't need much encouragement. She loves music and always seems to be moving to a beat.

Movement of Life

Twirling, whirling,
Dancing, prancing,
Walking, talking.
All of life is moving, grooving
To the beat of life.

Life is about going forward and living life to the fullest. We are meant to take care of ourselves and make the most of ourselves.

Rule #9: Celebrate Your Victories

We look for small victories every day. Did Elizabeth have a letterboard conversation with one of her friends at school? Did she do well at her speech therapy session? Did she try a new vegetable today? Did she get through math without throwing the calculator? Each of these victories helps tear down an obstacle in Elizabeth's path.

These celebrations would not have been possible without the constant support of my own dear mother, Mimi, a How Person to be sure. We spend a lot of time at Mimi's house on the lake where I grew up. Mimi has been there for me, cheering our daily victories as well as cleaning up the messes. Sometimes the days get long, and it helps to have Mimi telling me that "this too shall pass." And those days do pass and better ones follow: days when we celebrate having a good day at school or learning to swim underwater. Mimi never looks backward, only forward. She says she doesn't have time for dwelling on the past. Instead, we take each day and celebrate our small victories.

Rule #10: Be a Victor, Not a Victim

Victor Frankl wrote about choosing happiness in his classic book *Man's Search for Meaning*. Frankl was an accomplished psychiatrist when he was sent to a concentration camp in Nazi Germany. During those terrible years, he was surprised to observe how some inmates survived and how others perished. His resulting philosophy concludes that we all have the choice, no matter how difficult our situation, whether to be victims or victors. It is beautifully fitting that Frankl's parents gave him the name that they did.

Frankl writes, "We who lived in concentration camps can remember the men who walked through the huts comforting others, giving away their last piece of bread. They may have been few in number, but they offer sufficient proof that everything can be taken from a man but one thing: the last of the human freedoms—to choose one's attitude in any given set of circumstances, to choose one's own way."[6]

Despite her trials, Elizabeth chooses to look on the bright side of life. She says of this poem, "**I wrote this acrostic poem at school. We were to use the word EMOTIONS. I chose to be positive and write about happy times. I like being happy and smiling.**"

E verything I feel

M y ups and downs

O ften feeling happy

T aking time to laugh

I feel good

O utside is fun

N ever be sad

S miling at people

In the concentration camp, Frankl saw how those who chose to be kind and positive were the ones who were more likely to survive (see Rule #1). They were relentless in their desire to live. So are we, for the sake of our children.

10

Middle School

Be Flexible

Nothing is more flexible or softer than water, yet nothing can resist it.

Lao Tzu

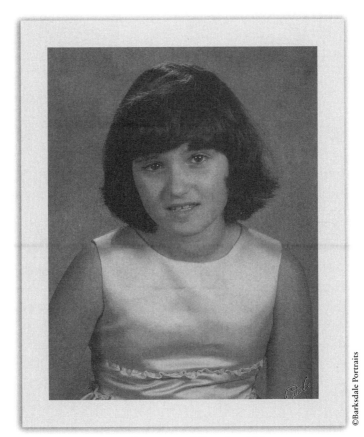

Right before my middle school blues

Turmoil

It is hard growing up.
My thoughts don't stop
Arguing and commenting
About my autism.
It is hard growing up.
Life is long and big.
My thoughts don't stop.

(age 12)

People don't get it! I have autism. I am different. I
am how God made me. I am acting like I do because
it is part of autism.

Middle school has given Elizabeth a whole new set of challenges. In the transition to adolescence, and from the very personal approach of elementary school to the more institutional approach of middle school, she has lost her footing and has frequent meltdowns. Elizabeth did well when a teacher was able to get to know her, but the middle school model of eight teachers for only forty minutes each day was not allowing them to understand her or her to understand them.

Because the middle school schedule was so stressful, we moved to more one-on-one instruction, but that also has a drawback: increased isolation. We asked Elizabeth why she said that school was hard for her, because she excels academically. She typed, "**I feel alone and I know it is going to be that way.**" Our plan had been to continue with mainstream education, but plans need to be flexible in autism land.

That reminds me of my middle school English teacher. On the first day of class he asked us what would be the most important thing that we could learn that year. Many enthusiastic hands shot up with answers like "how to be a good writer" and "to appreciate literature." Wrong, wrong. His answer was: learn to be flexible. He said that life would throw us curveballs, and we had a choice to be flexible and roll with the punches or to be rigid and end up broken. At the time I thought that he was giving us vocational advice, saying that we needed to prepare for

multiple careers during our lifetime. Now I wonder if he had a child with autism.

Despite our desire for Elizabeth to succeed in mainstream school, we have to be careful not to put too much pressure on her. She wrote this poem when she felt the pressure of four days of New Jersey state testing (the New Jersey Assessment of Skills and Knowledge test or NJ ASK) weighing on her:

School Days

First day of school,
So many rules.
A teacher that yells
Instead of tells.
Lunches so loud
My head pounds.
All the lunch aide does is frown.
NJ ASK testing
On a lot the scores are reflecting.
"Last day is here!"
I say this with good cheer.

I have been blessed with people who have worked with me, but some people are not as compassionate or understanding as others. I was extremely stressed when preparing for state testing. I felt fear and stress in the classroom air.

On a recent visit with Soma, we used our time trying to figure out how to make middle school tolerable for Elizabeth:

Mom: Do you think that we will be able to make school work? Terri is walking on eggshells every day because of your behavior.

Elizabeth: **She is walking on water. It is God's wish I am with Terri.**

Soma: Yes, you are very lucky to have Terri. She is very patient with you.

Elizabeth: **It is one thing to be patient and another to get bored in school.**

Soma: Tell me three ways to make school better.

Elizabeth: **Try imagining I am not there if I bang my head. Try to talk softly to me and around me. Try to make me do projects instead of sitting and listening. Like I can do history projects.**

Soma: Do you mean doing something on the computer?

Elizabeth: **No, it is more like making a booklet.**

Soma: I understand. Is it that the teacher talks and it becomes like "*wah, wah, wah*"?

Elizabeth: **Yes, I can't hear at a stretch. I don't mind school if I get more breaks.**

Soma: Would you like to go for a walk and get some fresh air?

Elizabeth: **Yes. How about some space in school? My body is so unpredictable.**

Soma: What else?

Elizabeth: **No tests. I don't like tests.**

In this conversation, I was struck with Elizabeth's juxtaposition of walking on eggshells with walking on water. Why would Elizabeth say that Terri walks on water? Is it because they have been together for almost a decade? Or is it because she came with us to Wisconsin in January when it was frigidly cold as we chased yet another "speech expert"? Is it that she read the entire Harry Potter series to Elizabeth in our HBOT (Hyperbaric Oxygen Treatment), a tubular oxygen chamber that is supposed to help Elizabeth detox but makes me squirm with claustrophobia? Or is it because Terri has stood by Elizabeth through it all? Yes, it is all this and more. In our home, Terri walks on water.

Elizabeth has asked us for a lot of flexibility, and we will try to make school as accommodating as possible. More walks, more projects, more silence. Of course, the "no tests" part of the request may be hard to accommodate.

Like all teenagers, Elizabeth needs to know where the boundaries are:

Limitations

I have to confess
I am in the midst
Of trying for boundaries
That need to exist.

In my changing life
If we are going to avoid strife
You have to set limits
And expect me to be
What you would like to see for me.

> Tell me, Mom, how to act. This is a hard age. I want
> to fit in and act like everyone else. People still look
> at me sometimes. Tell me why.

In many ways, Elizabeth is a typical teenager. She tests the limits we set. She is trying to understand herself. However, her exploration has the complexity of autism mixed in, and that induces additional angst.

Elizabeth: **I want to know more about my condition.**

Soma: About autism?

Elizabeth: **How do they label?**

Soma: There are characteristics, and if you have eight out of twenty, you get the label. Most people have some of them.

Elizabeth: **It is not fine to judge.**

Sometimes Elizabeth shocks me with her worldliness. Despite appearances, our children hear everything going on around them. In a recent conversation with Soma, Elizabeth sets out to expand her literary ambitions by writing a play. In it, she reminds me that she is growing up fast.

Elizabeth: **I want to write plays.**

Soma: What kind? Happy ones, for movies?

Elizabeth: **That will be wonderful.**

Soma: Okay. So let's do an exercise with some dialogue. What is the scene?

Elizabeth: **Café, and through the window see a street.**

Soma: Okay, who is in the café?

Elizabeth: **Three girls.**

Soma: Their names?

Elizabeth: **Finch, Gina, and Europa.**

Soma: Okay, now some dialogue.

Elizabeth: **Gina: "My boyfriend is not in town."**

Europa: **"Is he joining the Marines?"**

Finch: **"Aren't you pregnant?"**

[*Big laughs from Soma and Mom.*]

Soma: Elizabeth, you will sell a lot of movies. You know what people are interested in.

With this play, Elizabeth is reminding me not to baby her. This is a big challenge for autism parents, especially if our children are nonverbal. We have to remember that they have the same teenage feelings and desires.

In a more recent visit with Soma, Elizabeth had the opportunity to visit with a handsome, seventeen-year-old young man who is also nonverbal. To see these two young people connect was magical. Elizabeth was not having a good morning, but Justin was not fazed and even tried to distract her by asking about something he thought all girls were interested in:

Justin: Elizabeth, I am Justin.

Elizabeth: *[Elizabeth came into the session upset, and she started to throw things.]* **I like drama.**

Justin: I like drama too.

Elizabeth: **It is hard with me to deal with life.**

Justin: Don't worry. You are trying your best.

Elizabeth: **It is hard to stay happy all the time.**

Justin: You have to make the best of it.

Elizabeth: *[still crying and throwing things]* **Not good to do what I do.**

Justin: Elizabeth, do you like shopping?

Elizabeth: **Nothing interests me much.**

Justin: I always thought that girls like it.

Elizabeth: *[calmer]* **I don't see the point in shopping.**

Justin: It needs to come from how much you have.

Elizabeth: **God wants us to be satisfied with little.**

Justin: Don't agree with that.

Soma: Justin wants to start his own business and make money.

Elizabeth: **I am writing poems.**

Justin: I can read them too.

Elizabeth: **Do you have a business?**

Justin: Soon I will. I am quitting school.

Elizabeth: **I am quitting too. It is not of my standard.**

Justin: It should be noisy.

Elizabeth: **Too many typical people. I feel alone.**

Justin: Yes. Typical people don't mix with us.

Elizabeth: **At first they try, then lose patience.**

This conversation tells me so much about Elizabeth in so few words. Like most adolescents, she is having a hard time coping with life. Sometimes she is angry and depressed, but she wants to pull herself out of it. She identifies herself as a poet and doesn't care about material things. She is not comfortable in

school because it is not designed with her needs in mind. Her inability to communicate verbally leaves her feeling isolated. It takes patience for talking people to get to know her, because it takes time for her to type out her responses. She wants us to take the time.

Bad Days

Things seemed strange at least to me.
My day was not going as it should be.
Things were different in an odd sort of way.
If you ask me how I could not say.
Was it better? We'll see
If it keeps happening to me.

Some days at school I am bored. I have to sit for long periods of time. I do not do artwork like coloring. I have a hard time cutting, and I answer questions slowly on my letterboard. Sometimes I am very frustrated.

Our children grow up, and despite their obstacles, we have hopes and dreams for them. Our dreams for Elizabeth include high school, college, and a happy life, however she ends up defining that for herself. Will we get there? If we manage to get through middle school, the rest will be a breeze.

11

Families

We All Have Our Stories

Happy families are all happy in the same ways.
Unhappy families are unhappy in their own unique ways.

Leo Tolstoy, *Anna Karenina*

With Charles and Gale at Christmastime

Thanksgiving

A very important time of year
All your family gathers near
Thankful for all that you hold dear.

Let God know
His blessings flow
Into your life like a beautiful rainbow.

(age 9)

Holiday thoughts about traditions and how they are
important to me.

Our family isn't normal. But what family is?"

Author Patsy Clairmont said it well: normal is just a setting on the dryer.

A family doesn't have to be normal (whatever that is) to survive and eventually thrive. The Bible is littered with families that are far from normal and yet produce the most remarkable people: Joseph's brothers sold him into slavery, and Jacob stole his brother's birthright. Our families hand us good and bad in one big package. They give us our dreams, our craziness, our drive to succeed. To embrace our family's craziness along with the goodness is to embrace the craziness and goodness in ourselves, which we turn around and give to our children.

We all have our stories. Our family seems to thrive on taking everything to an extreme. One piece of our family lore concerns Elizabeth's great-great-grandmother (my mother's father's mother) who was left with five children when her husband died in the influenza pandemic of 1918. She tried hard to make ends meet but was forced to send three of her boys, including my grandfather, whom we call Pop, to an orphanage. When Grand-Nana was about to be evicted, she solved that problem by marrying the landlord. She got her boys back but was forced to live with a crazy man who rebuilt his Model T every weekend.

I suspect that Elizabeth gets most of her brainpower from Pop. Despite his lack of a formal education beyond the eighth grade,

Pop loved reading and learning. Much of his vast vocabulary was gleaned from the *Reader's Digest* Word Power games, which he made me do religiously.

My earliest memory of Pop is listening to him read *Alice's Adventures in Wonderland*. The magic in that book has influenced how I look at the world and its infinite possibilities, even when I've gone through the looking glass into the alternative reality of autism. In fact, it's become even more meaningful to me as Elizabeth and I have journeyed through autism land, a frightening and often baffling world where logic seems to have been suspended.

Like Alice, we're doing our best to find our way home. When we stumble across something that says "drink me" or "eat me," we often do, hoping this will finally be the key to our escape. But just as Alice doesn't know what will happen to her when she drinks the potion, we don't always know how Elizabeth will react to a new medication, despite consulting with numerous doctors.

In one case, burned forever in my mind, it took us four doctors and six hormone interventions to find the right one for Elizabeth. After five terrible reactions where she would bang her head with escalating intensity, we found a specialist in Dallas who did a nonroutine blood test which finally led to an effective treatment. I remember the doctor saying, "If either of our hormone levels were four times higher than normal and you gave us one of those medications, we'd be banging our heads too!"

That's why they call medicine a "practice." It isn't perfect.

Some days when I'm making appointments with doctor after doctor, I feel like the Mad Hatter. When will this madness stop? When will Elizabeth be well? Then I look out our window and see the wildflowers dancing in the sunlight in the field where Elizabeth and I walk, and I think of the song from Disney's

Alice in Wonderland movie that tells us, "You can learn a lot of things from the flowers."[1]

Pop loved to pick beautiful bouquets of wildflowers on his daily walks. Purple and white violets, happy daisies, yellow dandelions, and delicate Queen Anne's lace filled numerous vases around our house. On special occasions when we discovered a new flower, I would sit on his lap and he would take out his antique magnifying glass and hold it for me to look through, saying, "See how perfect God made this little flower."

I carry on that tradition with Elizabeth on our walks, and just as the song says, I have learned a lot from flowers. Silent and beautiful like Elizabeth, they weather droughts and storms. Tiny buttercups relentlessly celebrate life, poking up from between the stones of our walkway and lifting their heads toward the sun.

Those flowers not only remind me of Pop, they also remind me that we, like Alice, will find our way home.

Escape

I looked down at the floor.
There was a magic door.
Everything in that place
Moved at a snail's pace.
I only want to go there
When I need a break!

Sometimes I feel that the world is moving so fast I can't keep up. It is so overwhelming at times. I do find myself shutting down at these times, and I want to be alone.

Not surprisingly, Pop loved people and would take the time to chat with those who crossed his path in life, particularly cashiers and waiters. I remember holding his large, calloused hand and walking to the penny candy store on Sunday mornings in the summertime. Ten cents would fill the small, brown paper bag with licorice, Tootsie Rolls, and gum. I suspect I got an extra piece of licorice because everyone loved Pop.

I was not surprised to read in the *Wall Street Journal* a few years ago that adults recall these simple one-on-one times as their most special childhood memories. It's not the big family ski vacation. It's reading a book with your grandpa. It's dinner out with your mom.

It's difficult to create these moments with Elizabeth. She has trouble sitting still and often doesn't want to be touched at all. On those rare occasions when she lets me hold her and sing a song or read a story, the time could not be more special. I've learned to savor these moments in the midst of the turmoil.

One of our special memories is the annual pilgrimage to the land of Mickey. Every year we request to stay in the same room at the Polynesian Resort, next to the pool with the volcano slide. Sameness is comforting for children with autism. Disney has made its parks workable for autism families by providing handicapped passes. Sometimes we get angry looks when Elizabeth and Charles bound down the handicap ramp, but waiting in line is just not possible for them.

Disney World

Disney World—the place to be.
Lots of fun for my family and me.
Happy memories to remember and share
With the people who were not there.

That is my happy place. I love spending time with my family here. It is a trip where I can anticipate the events. It is a tradition. I feel comfortable with traditional family trips.

In spite of those moments of peace in the Polynesian pool, the turmoil of autism ruled our lives. Ray "retired" from an exciting Wall Street career and gave up many of his Harvard dreams after we burned through seven nannies in two months. We measured their endurance in days. I remember one of them saying, "I don't know what's wrong with these kids. I say, 'Charles, Elizabeth, come here,' and they run the other way."

We didn't know why the children were "misbehaving" because their autism had not yet been diagnosed. One of us had to try to bring order to the chaos, and Ray volunteered.

"I have a career," he said. "You have a commitment."

Ray was referring to my ten-year commitment to manage the money invested in a new venture capital fund. Although he was leading a strategic technology initiative at a major Wall Street investment bank, he figured his colleagues could get by without him. If I quit, my investors would be abandoned.

These agonizing choices lie at the heart of any family's struggle with autism. The question is never who sacrifices but rather how will the sacrifices be apportioned. Ray's commitment to the kids has allowed me to keep my commitment to my investors, which in turn has given us the ability to bear the financial burden faced by all families dealing with autism.

In the dozen years since that fateful day, Ray has brought consistency for the children, allowing me the flexibility to travel for my work and for all those doctor appointments and teacher

meetings. He has also been active in a number of organizations in our community, including spearheading a bimonthly, non-denominational church service for children with special needs, called All God's Children.

The other member of our family who has been greatly affected by Elizabeth's and Charles's autism is their older sister, Gale. Currently a junior in high school, Gale excels in academics and loves playing her baritone in marching, concert, and jazz bands. Off the field, she marches to the beat of a different drummer, and we celebrate that she has found a group of quirky friends who love her. I just wish that they didn't text her so much.

Because of the needs of her siblings, Gale became independent at an early age. Despite our home being filled with ABA teachers day and night, Gale learned to do her elementary school homework without much assistance. By middle school, she was readily making her own dinner and doing her own laundry.

In order to make sure that Gale didn't get lost in the shuffle, I instituted "Gale Time" shortly after her siblings were diagnosed. On Sunday evenings Gale and I would go out to dinner. She chose the restaurant and the topics of conversation. As she got older, our Gale Time got squeezed by her time with friends. Now I joke with her, saying, "What about my Gale Time?"

As a parent, I've made a lot of mistakes, but Gale Time was *not* one of them. It gave me the precious gift of quiet time with a strong-willed child who is now a beautiful, confident young lady.

Because she sees what Charles and Elizabeth face on a daily basis, Gale has compassion for those who are different and is a natural peacemaker. She embraces her brother and sister and gracefully accepts the challenges they have brought into her life. Most seventeen-year-olds wouldn't even consider letting their fourteen-year-old brother hang out with their friends, but

Gale welcomes Charles despite his social awkwardness. I love it when they play Rock Band on our game system together—Gale on guitar, Charles on drums, and a dozen friends singing their hearts out.

Gale sometimes joins Elizabeth and me for walks. Last summer, Elizabeth got upset during a walk around Mimi's lake, and out of frustration, she angrily grabbed my hair in one hand and Gale's hair in the other. It burned like bee stings. Trying to pry each of her fingers open, I was about to lose my temper when I heard Gale gently telling her sister, "It will be okay, Elizabeth. It will be okay." Understanding born of love. Tears welled up in my eyes.

Most of my own childhood is a big blur punctuated by bizarre and special events, not unlike my life now as an autism mom. I remember the night that we packed up one of our four pet shops in a local strip mall. The dogs, cats, snakes, monkeys, alligators (pet shops had many exotic animals back then), rabbits, hamsters, fish, parrots, and other critters were all in a tizzy as we loaded them into the U-Haul. I guess there was some dispute with the landlord, but to my eight-year-old mind, it seemed like we were stealing our own stuff.

I have memories of my dad taking me to Las Vegas when I was ten years old. I stood on the side and counted cards while he sat at the blackjack table. Back then there was only one deck, or maybe two, in the shoe, and we had a system of hand signals worked out for hitting and holding. I remember enjoying some fine dinners from our winnings on that trip.

Fire punctuates my childhood memories. My dad loved the excitement of being a volunteer fireman in our town. He would eagerly jump out of bed when the siren blared and race to get behind the wheel of the ladder truck. Dad also liked to shoot off

fireworks, and Independence Day for us was filled with hysterics and hysteria. (The hysteria coming from my mother when a flare ended up on the roof.) One year for my birthday, dad showed up with a cake full of sparklers, which quickly turned the icing into a gray, gritty mess. In our family, the sight of a birthday cake elicits calls of "Get the sparklers!"

My dad worked hard, played hard, and, sadly, smoked too many cigarettes. He died of lung cancer at sixty-two, just months before the children were diagnosed with autism. My mom says that it was probably better that way because it would have crushed him. Although I miss him dearly and know he would have been so proud of Elizabeth's courage, perhaps it is better that he is spared the pain of this journey. And whenever Elizabeth shows her daredevil side, I have to smile because I can see my father's spirit of adventure living on in her.

Shortly after my dad's death, Mom sold their final and most successful business, an antique cooperative. Her retirement allows her to help us with the children. We try to schedule one special trip each year to thank her. Because we share a love of foreign cultures, our adventures have included Bermuda, England, a riverboat cruise down the Rhine, France, the Kingdom of Bhutan, sailing a catamaran down the Dalmatian Coast of Croatia, and a safari in East Africa. In every case Mom, just like Pop, made friends of the waiters, the bus drivers, and especially our hunky Croatian skipper.

My most special childhood memory of Mom is her reading me *Cheaper by the Dozen*. This true story of a family with a dozen children had quite an effect on my mom and, consequently, me. The Gilbreth family's father was an efficiency expert and used his methods to run every aspect of their household. Even their bathroom time was not wasted. The children were required to

turn on a tape recorder while on the toilet and learn French. By the end of the book, all the children were fluent. If you add it up, you will be surprised how much time you spend in the bathroom. You too could be fluent in French.

Mom's form of efficiency is a can-do attitude, which is my constant support in the autism fight. Ever since I was a child, she has believed in me. When I had crazy dreams of going to Harvard (my parents were woodworkers in our basement at the time), she said, "Of course you'll go to Harvard." It didn't matter that no one in our family had ever gone to college, let alone the Ivy League. It didn't matter that they didn't have the money for college; we would find a way somehow.

Today she believes that we will conquer autism, and with her wind beneath my wings, I believe we will as well. Pop and Mom are the How People of our family. They supported my dreams, and I will do my best to pass that spirit on to Elizabeth, whatever her dreams may be.

12

Suffering

A View from Tibet

Success is not final, failure is not fatal: it is the courage to continue that counts.

Winston Churchill

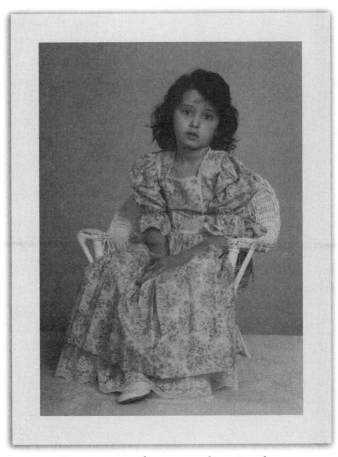

A vacant stare from my early autism days

Make a Change

Shades of gray
Like a cloudy day.
Things going on in the world
They make my mind whirl.
What will become of the world as we know it
If someone doesn't stand up and show it?
We need peace
And the wars to cease.
Can I be that one?
I need a voice to get it done.

(age 10)

When I wrote this poem I wanted to declare my position on war. I am for world peace. I will speak out for peace and an end to war. I plan to make a change in the world.

I still remember the horror on my father's face when he came home from our family's deli one night and said that a customer had heard I was telling the other children in school that I was an atheist.

To make a long and winding road short, I was raised in a nominally Christian home with a Catholic father and Protestant mother, and I fell away from my faith as a young girl when we stopped going to church. I came back to Christianity through the study of the world's other great religions. One of the most important times of my life was a year on a fellowship studying Eastern philosophies in Southeast Asia after college. As a result, you could say that my spiritual life, while Christian, is on the mystical side.

And Tibet is a mystical place.

In 1987, I found myself wandering around those enchanting mountain peaks. As I sat on the floor of the Jokhang Buddhist temple, packed among the local pilgrims, with only yak-butter candles lighting the quiet darkness, I could feel time stand still. Sometimes in the chaos of autism, I think about that stillness and try to feel that kind of peace again.

My time in Tibet made me think about how incomprehensible God is, how we can feel lost in the infinite vastness of the Maker of the universe, the One who is before time and beyond time. Tibet's snowcapped mountains are virtually untouched

by modern civilization. It's easier to feel God through nature in mountains of such vast beauty. Psalm 19:1 says, "The heavens declare the glory of God, and the sky above proclaims his handiwork" (ESV), so maybe Tibet, averaging 16,000 feet in altitude, *does* in some sense bring us closer to God in a way that standing on a stepladder couldn't.

In those mountains I felt small, and it reminded me that despite our best efforts to understand the nature of God, we are like ants contemplating the universe. Albert Einstein wrote, "My religion consists of a humble admiration of the illimitable superior spirit who reveals Himself in the slight details we are able to perceive with our frail and feeble minds."[1]

The Hawk

I saw a hawk.
Did he see me?
Each of us questioning
How it should be

For me to be him
And him to be me.
Flying up so very high
Watching as life goes by.

People are always thinking about how things should be better. Some even wish they were someone else. Everyone deals with different challenges. We have to appreciate people and their life journeys no matter what they might be.

From her first conversations with Soma, we learned that Elizabeth contemplated God and humanity's relationship to the divine in a way that went beyond what she learned in Sunday school. In 2006, at our third camp with Soma, Elizabeth was asked what she would like to talk about, and she replied, "**Tookie Williams.**" I was shocked. Days before, Tookie had been executed for multiple murders in spite of his profession of innocence and faith as well as his work toward ending gang violence, which earned him nominations for the Nobel Peace Prize.

> Mom: What do you want to know about Tookie Williams?
>
> Elizabeth: **Can he be with God?**
>
> Mom: [*long pause as I search for an answer*] No one knows exactly what happens after we die, but I believe that he is probably with God because he tried to be a good man in the end.
>
> Elizabeth: **Same place as Grandpa. He is so scared now that Tookie is there too. They shouldn't have let Tookie inside.** [*Her paternal grandfather had just passed away that month.*]
>
> Mom: It's okay, Elizabeth. Grandpa will be fine because no one is hurt when they are with God. We're talking about God a lot. Do you want to go to church?
>
> Elizabeth: **Can I be Jewish?**
>
> Mom: Why do you want to be Jewish?
>
> Elizabeth: **They have a good bonding with God. I am not seeing God now.**

Mom: [*another pause*] That's okay, Elizabeth. We spend our whole life looking for God.

Elizabeth's ability to plumb the depths of life is, at times, arresting:

Cycle of Life

Today is yesterday's growing up,
And it is the same sun rising up.
It never ends.
The cycle of life
With the good and the strife,
We all must take this journey.
That is what life is all about.

Life is a journey. We all must take it. Do the best that you can.

During my year studying in Southeast Asia, I learned about the cycle of life. Suffering is a central theme of Tibetan Buddhism, and in a way, it is relevant to any family fighting the scourge of autism. Buddhism's Four Noble Truths comprise the essence of the Buddha's teachings: (1) the truth of suffering, (2) the truth of the cause of suffering, (3) the truth of the end of suffering, and (4) the truth of the path that leads to the end of suffering.

M. Scott Peck translated this great truth in his simple yet profound statement "Life is difficult." In *The Road Less Traveled,* Peck continues: "This is a great truth, one of the greatest truths. It is a great truth because once we truly see this truth, we

167

transcend it. Once we truly know that life is difficult—once we truly understand and accept it—then life is no longer difficult."[2]

Life's Struggles

In a tunnel dark and dreary
Then I start to feel very weary.
All of a sudden I see a light
And then I start to feel all right.
Life is full of twists and turns,
Getting ahead and being burned.
Experience is the only way to learn.

Sometimes life is tough. We even struggle to do the things we love, even writing poetry.

As a young theology student, Rabbi Harold Kushner struggled with the idea of suffering as presented in the book of Job. But it was not until he was told that his three-year-old son, Aaron, would die of a rare disease by his early teens that he felt suffering's grip on his heart.

After Aaron's death, Rabbi Kushner tried to make sense of his own suffering as well as suffering in the world by writing *When Bad Things Happen to Good People*. He recognized the great chasm that suffering can create between ourselves and God as well as between ourselves and our loved ones. This passage from its introduction resonates in my soul:

I would write [this book] for all those people who wanted to go on believing, but whose anger at God made it hard for them to

hold on to their faith and be comforted by religion. And I would write it for all those people whose love of God and devotion to Him led them to blame themselves for their suffering and persuade themselves that they deserved it.[3]

This passage means so much because it speaks to two fundamental issues that autism parents want to be assured of: (1) God loves us, and (2) autism isn't our fault. God isn't punishing us or our children. We are not to blame for our child's illness. Some combination of genetic predisposition and environmental triggers led to this suffering in the world. God is in the midst of it, but how?

The suffering of the innocent poses a great challenge for anyone who believes in God, because it has a tendency to force us to choose, consciously or unconsciously, between two equally unattractive ways of thinking about God: If suffering is beyond God's control, is God really all-powerful? Or, if God wants the innocent to suffer, is God really good? We want God to make sense to us, to behave in conformity to our expectations. We don't want to choose between an ineffective God and an uncaring one.

In the end, though, God can't be defined by the limitations of our expectations. We see this in the book of Exodus. When Moses asks God what his name is, God simply replies, "I AM WHO I AM" (3:14). We try our best to explain God or put the divine in a logical box, but God's vastness surpasses our limited human capacity. I want God to be both all-powerful and all-good as I understand those terms. We all want God to be a lot of things, but God tells us, "I am who I am."

So why does God allow suffering in the world? I don't know, but I believe that God sees our suffering and feels our pain. God did not leave us here to wallow alone in meaningless despair.

"Likewise, the Spirit helps us in our weakness; for we do not know how to pray as we ought, but that very Spirit intercedes with sighs too deep for words" (Rom. 8:26 NRSV). On many days, my prayers are more sighs than words.

Since leaving Harvard, I have grown more comfortable admitting to my ignorance, sometimes several times a day. The Harvard ethos is much more "fake it till you make it." Any crack in the know-it-all façade was an invitation for a verbal tar-and-feathering. Saying "I don't know"—well, think of a shark tank at feeding time.

I now realize that my mind is not capable of even asking the right questions about God. I don't think I am ever going to understand why there is suffering in the world. For me, the allegory of the good mother and her baby enables me to make some sense of our suffering. It goes like this: The baby often can't understand why the good mother does what she does. The baby may scream with unhappiness, but the good mother has a plan and has her reasons. The good mother's plan, however, doesn't mean that the baby doesn't have the ability to make choices. When the baby makes a bad choice, the good mother weeps.

Elizabeth doesn't just question suffering in the world; she wants to take a stand to end it. When Elizabeth was in third grade, Terri told us that she started sobbing in school for no apparent reason. After school we asked her to write a poem about what she was feeling. This is what she wrote:

Your Insides

A cry, a tear,
A trail of fear.
The pain inside
Too strong to hide.
A sigh,
Oh my.
Why?

For months it tore me up that her autism was causing her such pain. Finally we asked her for an explanation, and she told us that it wasn't about her suffering at all:

> When I wrote this poem I was inspired by the war in Iraq. As children growing up in the United States we don't hear bombs or guns firing. I feel a terrible sadness in my heart for these children who live in fear and don't know why.

Recently Temple Grandin asked Elizabeth how she, as a person with autism, might perceive the world differently. Elizabeth responded, "**I am more sensitive to what is going on around me. I feel others' pain and suffering.**"

In her poem "Make a Change" at the beginning of this chapter, Elizabeth tells us that she needs a voice to be heard. She wants to advocate for peace and for war to cease. As part of our effort to give her a voice, we were able to highlight her poetry in a PBS television segment on *Religion & Ethics Newsweekly*

in October 2009. The roots of that show began in Tibet more than twenty years earlier.

During three months of wandering in China, I thought that my Buddhist studies would benefit from a side trip to Tibet. At the airport in Chengdu, China, I was lost in the large crowd of locals milling around until I spied one other *gweilo* (roughly translated "foreign devil") who looked hopelessly frustrated at the ticket counter.

I propped my large, external-frame backpack against the wall and wandered over. This gentleman had a ticket to fly to Tibet on the same flight as mine, but he didn't speak a word of Chinese, so for him, no seat was available. By this time, traveling alone, I had picked up enough Mandarin to manage basic travel talk. ("Where is the toilet?" "Can I buy one ticket to Tibet, please?" "Could I have the chicken, not dog, thank you?")

The stranger, who introduced himself as Charlie, did not seem to have much confidence in my meager language abilities but figured that he had nothing to lose. After many repetitions of "thank you so very, very much" and "you are so very, very kind," the gentleman had his seat.

A few hours later, I arrived in an exotic land and settled into the cheapest hotel in town. The electricity was sporadic and the hot water nonexistent, but I met a new friend, Hayes, and we enjoyed exploring the city's temples and bazaars. A few days later, Hayes and I ran into my airport friend, Charlie, in the main square, and he revealed that he was a producer with NBC News, scouting a story for Tom Brokaw. He had a driver, interpreter, and guide with him and invited us to join him for a day-trip to visit a Buddhist lama living in a mountainside cave.

To top it off, Charlie had a golden ticket: a set of Polaroid photos of himself with the Dalai Lama, the exiled king and god

of Tibetan Buddhism. The Dalai Lama fled Tibet in 1959 after the Chinese army invaded and took control. Even though he lives in exile in India, the Dalai Lama is still revered in Tibet. Everyone we met, whether monks in temples or herders tending their yaks, pressed the photos to their foreheads and opened their hearts to Charlie. No topic was off-limits.

During the Cultural Revolution, thousands of Buddhist monks were imprisoned or killed. Others were forced to marry and find a civilian occupation. In one isolated village, Charlie asked a former monk, "Would you go back to being a monk if they allowed it?"

Without hesitation, with his wife within earshot, he answered, "Yes!"

I witnessed enough of this heartfelt honesty to solidify my connection with both those Buddhist monks and this Irish-Catholic TV producer.

Our lives spun in separate orbits, but Charlie and I stayed connected over the years through occasional emails and phone calls. When he retired from NBC, I asked him if he could help me produce a couple of YouTube videos focused on Elizabeth's poetry. I hoped they might inspire other autism parents and their children. Instead, Charlie went one better. He, an Emmy Award–winning crew, and correspondent Bob Faw put together a beautiful PBS story that can still be viewed by visiting the PBS *Religion & Ethics Newsweekly* website and searching for "autistic poet."

Who knew that a chance meeting on "the roof of the world" would help give my daughter a voice more than twenty years later?

After the show aired, Charlie exchanged emails with Elizabeth to get her reaction. As usual, she said a lot with few words in the following exchange:

Charlie: How did being on film for PBS make you feel?

Elizabeth: **Seen in a new light.**

Charlie: What message are you trying to convey to the public?

Elizabeth: **Normal in here.**

Charlie: What is your biggest struggle?

Elizabeth: **Not talking.**

Charlie: What has been your greatest success?

Elizabeth: **My love of poetry.**

Charlie: Who do you feel understands you the most?

Elizabeth: **Mom.**

Charlie: What would you like the public to know about you?

Elizabeth: **I am in here.**

I believe that Elizabeth's voice—her speaking voice—will come. I believe that God is healing her. It remains a mystery to me why there is so much suffering in the world and why, despite our prayers, Elizabeth continues to drink from that cup.

13

God

Learning Each Other

To love another person is to see the face of God.

Les Misérables, the musical

Quiet walks with Mom

God Loves Us All

It does not matter who you are
It does not matter if you stray far
God is always there for you
In spite of what you may do
His love is stronger than anyone can know
You just have to know to go
to God.

(age 9)

I wrote this poem because I want people to know the power of faith. No matter what you face in your life—sickness, hunger, poverty, or just not having a relationship with God—he is always there for anyone who calls on him.

How can we know God?

It seems like such a simple question, but it usually takes a lifetime to answer, if we answer it at all. It goes beyond the basic question of deciding whether or not God exists. While faith is sometimes seen as the end of a journey, in reality, it's only the beginning. Those of us who have experienced enough of God's presence to be convinced of God's existence are confronted daily with a dizzying array of questions that never confront the nonbeliever: What does it mean to know God? How do I love somebody I can't even see? How can I experience God's presence in the midst of suffering?

While the answers to these questions are far beyond the scope of this book, one question has particular resonance with the autism struggle: How can we know God?

While this question may seem unconnected to autism, I believe it is a vital key to understanding our children. In his book *Living Jesus: Learning the Heart of the Gospel*, Luke Timothy Johnson argues that we cannot know another person in the same way that we know the state capitals or how to ride a bike. People aren't facts or static objects that can be fully mastered. Instead, we are constantly changing and growing beings who must be continually learned, with respect and attentiveness. We are mysteries to be experienced, not problems to be solved. Elizabeth's best teachers view her in this way. Because our children are so

different, this learning takes extra effort. But even the smallest learning can bring great joy.

If this is true with regard to relatively simple human beings, Johnson observes, how much more so for the infinite God, whose presence surrounds us and yet can seem so impenetrable and unfathomable at times? How much greater must our attentiveness be with God, whom we often experience indirectly and whose ways are a mystery to us?

This orientation has helped me be more at peace with the mysteries in life, especially with autism. Our children's interior worlds often remain a mystery. Yet this does not condemn us to being strangers, forever staring at each other across a yawning and unbridgeable chasm of silence. Rather, it simply means that we must use the same degree of care to learn our children that we use in our efforts to learn God.

Johnson states that the path of learning another person is founded on trust and respect. Without them, the person being learned is reduced to an object. Built on this foundation is attentiveness. He writes:

> Attentiveness suggests alertness, yes, but also receptivity. It is a "leaning toward" the other. Attentiveness is present when we truly listen to the other person, when we contemplate the other person. It does not assume that the other is already known, has been "figured out." Instead, it assumes that the other is always capable of change and surprise.[1]

What a beautiful notion of love and friendship and parenting and marriage: to lean toward the beloved and listen for a new surprise. If we are not vigilant, the world will conveniently put a label on our children and stop listening to them. I, like so

many other autism moms, know that they are full of surprises. Elizabeth has an opinion about nearly everything, but we need to draw out her viewpoint. She doesn't volunteer it. We must lean in and listen.

Johnson goes on to talk about patience as a necessary component of personal learning and how patience goes hand in hand with suffering. For any parent, patience is a virtue. For autism parents, it is a necessity. Our children do things for a reason, but it takes patience to learn the reason. Despite the exhaustion and frustration we feel from hearing the same phrase over and over again or seeing the same spinning or twirling action over and over, there is a reason, and we must try to learn our children if we are to help them.

A handful of authors with autism have helped autism parents get an inside look at their children. Temple Grandin's *Thinking in Pictures* and *The Way I See It* describe her need for deep pressure from a self-designed squeeze machine and how noncotton clothing was horribly itchy. In his book *The Mind Tree*, Soma's son, Tito Mukhopadhyay, wrote about how he could only feel his body in space by spinning it in circles.

In learning other people, including our difficult-to-learn children, with trust, respect, attentiveness, patience, and suffering, we also have a process to learn God. The spark of the divine in each of us brings us into the mystery of the divine. Elizabeth has always had a keen sense of God within:

God's Love

There is a light at my inside.
Sin is not in me.
To see God in a rose.

I am a believer. God lives in me. I am a Christian.
I know not to sin. God is the maker of all things.
That means they are beautiful.

Spirituality is a deep current in the autism community. In *Autism and the God Connection,* William Stillman, himself on the autism spectrum, chronicles the spiritual side of numerous children and adults with autism. He found their spiritual sensitivity extended to the physical world around them. People with autism tend to have acute senses of smell, hearing, touch, and sight. A slight sound or faint light can immediately catch their attention.

One of my favorite stories is about a young man named Josh who is tall and thin with red-gold hair and refined features. Josh is nonverbal and has lived in a group home most of his life. When he turned twenty-one, he was no longer eligible for services and needed to move to a new group home. Josh was fine with the move, but after about a month, he was waking up in the middle of the night screaming in fear.

The beauty of this story is what the staff didn't do. They didn't write it off as part of his autism and medicate or restrain him. They believed, as I passionately do, that people with autism do things for a reason. They brought in an expert, Stillman, to try to figure out why Josh was in a constant panic.

Josh typed out for him "ghost" and then went on to describe in detail three figures that came to his room in the night. One was named Edward and had a beard, one was Sarah, and one named Samuel was twenty-one years old. Josh indicated that they were coming from a small, 1800s-era cemetery on an adjacent property. Although Josh was always with his caretakers at his group home

and had never visited the cemetery, the names matched three of the headstones, including Samuel, who died at age twenty-one. Stillman concluded that Josh's extreme sensitivity allowed him to feel the energy of these spirits.[2]

I believe that Elizabeth has some of the same extreme sensitivity to sense God in the world around her. We have tried to encourage her spiritual development by taking her to church and reading a wide variety of books to her, but her spirituality goes beyond this. Elizabeth discusses the difficulty of learning God with earthly distractions all around us:

Elizabeth: **Most of our nature is to distract us from God. Can you define God?**

    Soma: I'm too small to define God. But can you define?

Elizabeth: **That is the trouble. He is too much. How many people know him?**

    Soma: Very few. He is mysterious. But mystery is beautiful too.

Elizabeth is right. In many ways, God *is* too much. In his book *The Silence of God*, James Carse writes about how we ask God to speak to us directly, but if that were to happen, we would be overcome by the sheer power of the word. We see this in the book of Exodus when Moses asks to see God's glory. God refuses, knowing it would be fatal for Moses. Instead, God puts Moses in the cleft of a rock and covers him with a divine hand. When God passes by, Moses can catch a small glimpse of God's glory without being overcome by it.

The psalmist wrote that God understands our weakness and remembers we are only dust. I believe that in compassion for our frailty, God has surrounded us with signs of divine

loving-kindness that are constant reminders of a holy presence strong enough to sustain us yet gentle enough not to overwhelm us. In a world of pressing demands and constant distractions, however, it is easy to overlook these quiet love notes from God.

The spiritual life is a journey of training ourselves to recognize God's presence as it permeates our world and becomes the background music of our lives. We need to learn to dance to the constant rhythm of God's love, in which we live and move and have our being. I believe Elizabeth is moving to this rhythm when she speaks about her love of music and its vibrations.

Sounds

I am always moving
To the beat of the sounds
That are all around.

Not everyone can hear
What seems so near
To me.

I am always moving
To the beat
That to me is neat.

I feel like my sense of hearing is much more sensitive than most other people's. I hear every hum, squeal, and squeak of a place or thing. Sometimes it is hard to sort all of it out.

As with all of us who are learning God, Elizabeth's under-standing has evolved over time. When she was eight years old, she had this view of God:

> After we finish living we go to God; otherwise it is not easy to go to God. But I don't like God to be so scary that he will get mad if we are wrong, and I think I try to love him but I can't because I can't actually love anyone who can send people to hell. But I am trying hard to love him so that I don't go to hell. But I am not dying now, for I am still little.

As an adolescent, her experience of God has grown more complex. Our relationships with God *are* personal and unique for each of us, just as our relationship with each of our children is personal and unique. I want to probe Elizabeth's spiritual side because she teaches me things when I listen closely to her words. Sometimes she rightfully tells me to leave her be:

Soma: How do you experience God?

Elizabeth: **I am hoping to find God but I feel his presence.**

Soma: How do you feel God's presence?

Elizabeth: **It is a private matter between me and God.**

The agonizing irony of Elizabeth's condition in the early years, before she could type on a letterboard, is that for all the noise and distraction she created, she was unable to communicate her simplest wants and needs to us and to express to us what was happening in her mind. We were separated by what seemed like

a deafening silence. In the words of novelist Michael O'Brien, our silences weren't speaking to each other.

What I needed to learn was that although silence could be a burden, it could also be an invaluable gift in learning my daughter. In a world that screams for our attention all day long, silence is a rarity. We talk more than we listen; in our noisy, distraction-driven culture, silence can be downright frightening. When we are face-to-face with the silence of another person, our thoughts often turn dark: "Are you angry with me? Disappointed? Don't you have anything to say to me?"

In his book *Celebration of Discipline: The Path to Spiritual Growth*, Richard Foster astutely observed that "the reason we can hardly bear to remain silent is that it makes us feel helpless. We are so accustomed to relying upon words to manage and control others. If we are silent, who will take control? God will take control, but we will never let him take control until we trust him. Silence is intimately related to trust."[3]

Years later, and now that Elizabeth can write her thoughts, she has taught me that sitting in silence can be beautiful. In the stillness, we can feel the love that we have for each other and feel God's presence. We are not two strangers poking at each other in the dark but two souls overlapping in quiet communion. As German philosopher Eberhard Arnold wrote in his article, "Why We Choose Silence Over Dialogue," "People who love one another can be silent together."[4]

My friend Cheryl and I are that way. We have been friends since we were eight years old, and we can talk for hours or just sit with each other in silence. In the course of our almost forty years of friendship, sometimes we haven't spoken for months. Then she senses that I need her, such as when my dad died and when the kids were first diagnosed with autism, and she calls

me. There is something that connects us beyond this world. She smiles when I call her my angel.

When we were young girls, we were fearless. Looking back at it now, it seems more like reckless. Roof badminton is a case in point. One sunny afternoon we were playing badminton in Cheryl's front yard when the birdie landed on the roof. Since it was our only one, we decided to go up and get it. Cheryl found a ladder and I climbed up. When I hit it down to her, she hit it back up to me, and roof badminton was born.

Whenever we had a chance, with decent weather and no parents in sight, one of us was on the roof serving that birdie. We would race back and forth practically diving for shots. Mind you, Cheryl lived in a modest, one-story ranch house, but at eleven years old, we thought it was the Empire State Building. It's a miracle that any of us survive childhood.

Our friendship over the years has been a roof badminton game over time and space. She has been there for me when I have been on the ground, and I have tried to be there for her when she was grounded. Like most childhood friends, we no longer live close to each other, so it has been a challenge to stay a meaningful part of each others' lives. Both of us juggled career and family obligations that had high levels of stress. Cheryl has two beautiful daughters, one also named Elizabeth. Until recently, she ran a nursing home where the patients adored her. She loved to listen to them and dance with them. Life-and-death stress was part of her work every day. She told me about how those with strong spiritual lives passed peacefully, holding her hands.

In the midst of the roof badminton game of life, where is the time for us to hold hands with our dear friends? At least today Cheryl and I have email and cell phones to help us hit the birdie back and forth. It's not quite the same as all-night talks

at our sleepover parties, but it gets us through the tough times. Recently she made me cry by sending a photo of the two of us in a frame that reads, "We will be an encouragement to each other. Romans 15:32." It sits on my desk and always makes me smile.

As children, Cheryl and I were not in school together because she went to the Catholic school in the next town over. We met on the diving team at our local YMCA. Each week we practiced on the trampoline and in the pool for many hours. We were fearless fancy divers.

Fearless until we had our accidents. At about the same time, Cheryl hit her leg doing an inward somersault, and I hit my face on the board doing a backward somersault. Cheryl's injury was more serious, but mine was more dramatic as the blood from my nose made the pool look like the shower scene in *Psycho*. After that we were no longer fearless but perhaps a bit wiser.

When I think back to that time on the diving board, it makes me think of the many dives we take in life—marriage and children being cliff dives. We dive into these commitments without knowing whether they will be full of beauty and grace or crashes on the board. Most of our dives, in life or on the board, are neither perfect nor disaster but somewhere in between. We survive the belly flops, bumps, and bruises. We try to learn from them.

Shortly after our last visit together, Cheryl was in a car accident. She was driving safely down the road when a random event happened: a car in the next lane slid over and knocked her into the median. A few days later, she called to tell me that she was a little shaken up but didn't appear to have any serious injuries. Then the pain came.

Despite being a nurse, she had a hard time getting some of the doctors to believe that she had an injury and was in pain. It reminds me of the plight of so many women with chronic

fatigue syndrome whose symptoms are often dismissed as psychosomatic. She could not sit and could only stand for short periods of time. She spent most of each day in bed.

I asked her what she did all day long. Did she read books or watch television?

She responded, "No, I mostly just try to quiet my mind." Then with a laugh she added, "I can kneel without much pain, so I guess that God wants me to do some praying as well."

For more than a year, she traveled from doctor to doctor, much like we have done in our autism journey. No one could put a name to it. No one could relieve her pain.

And in all that time of lying in bed in pain, I never heard her complain once. Not once.

She told me that God was slowing her down. She needed this time to be silent. To listen for that still, small voice.

Finally Cheryl found a doctor who gave her suffering a name: pudendal neuralgia. Basically, a nerve in her backside was being pinched by a fibrous mass. People are often misdiagnosed for years and don't like to speak about it because they are embarrassed by its symptoms. Pudendal neuralgia is rare, and it resigns most to a lifetime of pain.

But Cheryl will not be discouraged. Her life is filled with a strict therapy schedule and lots of prayer. She says she knows God is healing her. In the midst of her days of quieting her mind, she prays for Elizabeth. I know because she sends text messages to tell me.

That is a How Person: someone who reaches beyond her own suffering to care about someone else's.

God

Two by two
It seemed so few.
God knew
What he had to do
To assure the fate
Of the human race.
We are so loved to have someone all knowing
To help keep the world going.

I am so glad that there is a spiritual being that loves us so. If we trust in him we will always be assured of unconditional support and guidance throughout our lives. God is good.

In her quiet time with God, Elizabeth offers her own prayers for those who are suffering: "**I am concerned about the war. Innocent people are dying. People should not have to suffer. I want peace. I try to show that when I write. If people are exposed to good and peaceful things, maybe they will be that way themselves. This is what I pray for at night.**"

It's amazing to me that at her young age, Elizabeth has already grasped that silence isn't merely the absence of words. It's the positive act of overcoming the distracting din of the world's constant babble.

Elizabeth reminds me that learning God is complex and simple at the same time. Consider this exchange:

Soma: Have you ever heard God speak to you?

Elizabeth: **It is not to be discussed.**

Soma: What is your philosophy about life?

Elizabeth: **Life is a riddle. It makes me wonder about everything.**

Soma: How do you feel God's love?

Elizabeth: **Most of God's love comes from Mom and Dad. The rest comes from knowing I am loved.**

So the question of how we know God comes full circle. Elizabeth has helped me realize that what began for me as an inwardly focused mystery is to an equal degree an outwardly focused calling. I know God most deeply when I am striving against my own limitations to bring God's love into the lives of others. I know God most fully when, in my darkest moments of doubt and despair, I am lifted up by the simple faith and kindness of those dearest to me.

I believe the burden of Elizabeth's autism has helped us both understand one of life's great mysteries: the most tangible way we experience the invisible God is through the presence of the people God has placed in our lives. If there is mystery in our spiritual journeys, there are also signposts along the way. For me, simple acts of kindness are moments in the presence of the divine.

One of the most profound statements I've ever heard about God is the most simple: God is love. It means that love isn't merely something God does, love is who God *is*. It is easy to sentimentalize these words, but to do so robs them of their power. The hard truth of love is that it doesn't consist primarily of long, hand-holding walks along a sunset beach. It consists of the small

acts of ever-deepening self-sacrifice that we undertake for the good of those we love.

This is especially true for autism parents. Our love for our children has called us to give of ourselves in ways we never could have imagined. There is nothing glamorous or sentimental about it. The seemingly endless stream of sleepless nights, tear-filled days, tantrums, doctors' appointments, and school meetings stretches us well beyond our breaking point. It is often lonely, thankless work, and we sometimes find ourselves feeling that it's all futile, as though we're pouring ourselves drop by drop into a bottomless hole, unnoticed by anyone.

But it is precisely in these unheralded acts of mercy that God is the closest to us. I believe God sees these hidden mercies, gathering them up and returning them to us in the form of the love and support of our friends and family. God returns them to us in the prayers others offer up to sustain us in our darkest hours. God returns them to us in the peace that passes all understanding.

14

Healing

A Wing and a Prayer

God, grant me the serenity
to accept the things I cannot change;
courage to change the things I can;
and wisdom to know the difference.
Living one day at a time;
enjoying one moment at a time;
accepting hardships as the pathway to peace.

Reinhold Niebuhr

In Seattle to see Pastor Bill

Mind

Inside my mind
I often find
An empty space
That needs a trace
Of something I can't
Quite put in words.
It's like a hole,
Dark and deep,
Waiting for the light
To seep
Within.

(age 9)

I struggle daily trying to make my mouth work like
everyone else around me. It's as if there is a missing
link that I cannot call on to make it happen. I am
trying more and more to get the words in my head
to come out of my mouth.

Halfway across the country, it occurred to me: What am I doing flying to Seattle with Elizabeth and Charles for healing prayer with a Lutheran minister I've never met?

It was September 11, six years after my frantic conversation with the nursery school director while planes crashed into the World Trade Center and the world was forever changed. And once again, I was living between two worlds—the physical and the spiritual, the brokenness and the healing, the already and the not yet.

It all started with a conversation with an old friend, Sean, whom I've known since high school, when we shared a rebel gene and a deep-seated aversion to authority. Sean was the one who introduced me to the concept of "Why People" and "How People." He developed it during his years working with homeless people, when he helped many people get back onto their feet and into the mainstream of society. He said the people who were obsessed with finding out *why* the injustices that resulted in their homelessness occurred had much greater difficulty moving forward. The people who were focused on *how* to move on, regardless of *why* they were homeless, were much more likely to regain their lives. Sean said he decided to make this attitude part of his own approach to life.

In many ways, though, he made that decision years before. Sean has a pronounced stutter, a speech impairment he's carried with him since childhood. Although Sean is brilliant, he didn't do

well in high school, falling between the cracks the way children with disabilities often do. In high school, Sean and I shared a love of literature, but he didn't study much, and he liked to tease me for being such a geek.

Sean didn't go to college upon graduation, choosing instead to take a blue-collar job where he didn't have to speak much while he pursued a career as a rock musician. After a few years, he realized he was at a crossroads. He could let his life, his work, and his future be defined by his disability, or he could figure out how to move forward regardless of his disability.

Sean chose to be a How Person.

For the next decade, Sean worked intensely to overcome his speech impairment. He went to college, where he graduated at the top of his class before going on to law school. Today we joke with Sean that it is difficult to get him to stop talking. He communicates with audiences both large and small as a corporate attorney, adjunct college professor, musician, and Sunday school teacher. When he speaks, you don't notice his disability. You listen to what he says, especially when he is telling one of his many Irish jokes.

Sean introduced me to healing prayer when Elizabeth was a toddler. He asked if he and his wife, Susan, could come down from Boston and pray for Elizabeth. I was a bit apprehensive at first, but I trusted Sean not to do anything that would be harmful in any way. When Sean and Susan arrived, we all sat and talked about our lives for a while.

As Elizabeth darted around the room, I reached out and pulled her up on my lap. "I know you're in there, honey," I said, touching my forehead to hers. "We're coming to get you." I put Elizabeth back down on the carpet, and we all knelt next to her as Sean placed his hands on her head.

"Elizabeth," he said softly, "God loves you. He knows you're hurting, honey. He sees your burden and wants to bear it for you." She sat still as he prayed over her. "God, please put your arms around Elizabeth right now, and let her know that you are here for her. Take this burden from her and heal her mind and body. We ask this in the name of the Father, the Son, and the Holy Spirit. Amen."

It was a short prayer, but it meant so much to me. I could tell that it meant a lot to Elizabeth as well, because she looked right into Sean's eyes for several seconds at the end. Like most children with autism, Elizabeth had great difficulty looking anyone in the eye. This was special. She was thanking Sean. She knew that help was on the way.

"God has big plans for Elizabeth," Sean said with a smile. "I don't know what they are, but I have a feeling they're going to be big."

"Bigger than we can imagine," I replied.

Years passed, and I dabbled in healing prayer, although I didn't think that I was dabbling. I was praying sincerely but ignorant as to how to pray effectively. Tired and depressed, I reached out to Sean over a cup of tea during one of my Boston business trips. "I've been praying for the children for so long. It seems like nothing is happening. I don't know what to do anymore."

Sean responded with an impish smile, "Why don't you do what you've done with all the educational and medical stuff? Stop messing around and learn from someone who actually knows what they're doing." A good place to start, he suggested, was Agnes Sanford.

Searching the internet, I found that Agnes had written many books on living a Spirit-filled life. She described herself not as a healer but as a teacher of healing prayer. Her belief in its power

came when she herself was healed of debilitating depression. In her own ministry, she started with small healings and grew to seeing countless gravely ill people healed by God.

Agnes told the story of volunteering as a Gray Lady in the Red Cross at the Tilton Army Hospital at Fort Dix during World War II. Her cart was stocked with candy, magazines, and cigarettes, but Agnes saw men suffering and had more than candy to give them. Because she was forbidden by hospital policy to talk about God, she told them about a power like electricity that could flow through her and make them well. Soldiers of all faiths listened to her quiet prayers, her hands gently touching their wounded limbs, hidden under a strategically placed comic book.

Agnes believed that we are all "children of the Light" who can be a channel for God's healing power. In her fascinating autobiography, *Sealed Orders*, she instructs us to start with small miracles and move to larger challenges as we grow spiritually. Don't start with cancer, Agnes suggests. Better to start with a missing credit card.

Taking Agnes's cue, my adventure in healing prayer started with a lost rodent. Somehow my niece's hamster got out of its cage while it was entrusted to my care. I had twenty-four hours before she would return to pick it up, and I prayed long and hard that God would send the little fur ball my way.

Praying is not easy for me. My mind often wanders. I pray for the children, and then I start thinking about my to-do list for them. This time I was really trying to focus on that hamster and nothing else.

All day long I prayed. I looked in the couches and under the couches. I looked under beds. I called the little bugger, as if it were a dog. I looked in closets and cabinets. I wandered around

the house like I was playing a game of hide-and-seek as I asked God if I was getting warmer or colder.

By the end of the day, I was exhausted. My niece was coming in the morning, and I had not even had a glimpse of the rodent. It was bedtime.

Bleary-eyed, I was in the bathroom, saying one last prayer, when I looked down and saw two beady, black hamster eyes looking up at me.

Slowly, I knelt down. I was close to victory, but it could scamper away at any moment. Ever so slowly, I cupped my hands around this wayward little fur ball.

Gotcha!

Who says God doesn't answer prayers?

My rodent victory gave me the encouragement to pray for bigger things. God seemed to be prodding me along like a toddler taking her first tentative steps. By trusting in God and receiving the answers to small prayers, we find the strength to pray and trust and wait on bigger things.

The waiting is the hard part for me. I have to remind myself that God is not a server at the local diner, waiting to take my order. Trust and relationship are built over time. If God sent a deluge of healing power through a channel the size of a straw, it would be swept away.

The problem is: I am that straw.

I had been praying for God to heal Elizabeth for a long time. The problem isn't God; it's just that my channel is only robust enough for missing rodents right now. As I am in the process of growing, I need the humility to reach out to others who are further developed. I need to take her to someone whose channel is bigger.

I suspected Agnes's channel was big enough for autism. We would go wherever she was. But with a trip to Wikipedia, I was

devastated to learn that Agnes passed away in 1982. Fortunately, we had a backup channel: Agnes had mentored a young Lutheran pastor named Bill Vaswig.

Pastor Bill came to know Agnes and her ministry when she healed his teenage son, Philip, of schizophrenia through prayer. Pastor Bill wrote about this healing in a marvelous little book called *I Prayed, He Answered*. Pastor Bill is now almost eighty years old and sees a small number of people, many of whom travel great distances.

One hot August afternoon, I anxiously dialed his number. What would I say to him? "I'm desperate for my children to be healed"? "Please, please, please help me"? "After a decade of trying everything, I am exhausted and can't take it much longer"?

As soon as he answered the phone, I was overcome with a sense of calm. He was warm and kind and listened to me ramble on about our journey, my faith in God, and how much I wanted the children to be well.

"What should we do now?" I asked. To my delight, he said to bring the children to Seattle so that we could pray for them. He said that he loved big challenges.

When I told Sean about all of this, he was overjoyed for us: we were going to see one of his beacons on this earth. Healing prayer had become even more important to Sean in those days. Tragically, his wife, Susan, had a massive stroke about two years after they prayed for Elizabeth. She was only thirty-eight. It was a devastating blow to her health and left her with a seizure disorder that had seriously impaired her life. In the years following her stroke, Susan and Sean had been to countless experts and hospitals across the country to try to make sure Susan was getting the best available care.

"Could you do me a favor, Ginnie?" Sean asked. "When you're out there in Seattle, could you please ask Pastor Bill if I could bring Susan sometime for him to pray over her too?"

"I'll call you right back," I said, hanging up the phone.

I couldn't make Sean and Sue wait. They were carrying a heavy burden as well.

I picked up the phone and sheepishly called Pastor Bill back. "Could I pile a brain injury on top of autism?" I asked. I explained how Sean had been the reason that I knew about Pastor Bill in the first place and that Susan needed prayer.

"No problem. I told you, I love big challenges."

I thanked him and called Sean right back. "Pack your bags, you're coming with us to Seattle."

After getting over his shock, Sean was thrilled. Despite the difficultly of traveling, Susan immediately agreed to go.

We met Pastor Bill at his tiny office in Issaquah, Washington. Sue and Sean stayed with Charles and Elizabeth so that I could have some quiet time with Pastor Bill.

A tall Norwegian with silver hair and a warm smile, Pastor Bill shook my hand and immediately asked me about the children. He wanted to understand autism so that he would know how best to pray for them. I tried to explain the biomedical issues and ended by reading some of Elizabeth's poems.

Pastor Bill asked to see each of the children individually to pray for them. Elizabeth was first. He stood behind her and I knelt in front. Pastor Bill gently placed his hands on Elizabeth's head and quietly prayed, "Dear God. You know Elizabeth. You made her. You love her. Can you put your arms around her now, Jesus? Can you let her know that you are here with her?"

Elizabeth looked up at Pastor Bill for a moment. He continued, "God, we lift up Elizabeth. We see her healthy and strong. We

see her body being healed of all its problems. We see her stomach being healed and her brain being healed. We don't know all the things that need to be healed, but you do, God. You know Elizabeth. We pray that your healing power comes into Elizabeth and heals her. We pray that she be healed and for her to speak. We pray these things in Jesus's name. Amen."

Elizabeth looked up again, but this time she jumped up and ran out the door. Good thing Pastor Bill likes big challenges.

Charles was next. We prayed for him to be able to learn more easily. We prayed for him to be healed. He was unusually calm during our prayers. Although he could not express it with his limited vocabulary, I believe Charles felt God's peace. Then Sue and Sean had their turn.

We did much of the same morning and afternoon for the next two days. We prayed for God to heal the children, to take away their physical and mental pain. We prayed for Elizabeth to speak and for Charles to understand. We prayed for whatever damage had been done to their bodies to be reversed. We laid our hands on them and prayed and prayed.

At the end of our visit, Pastor Bill and I again had some quiet time. It had been a lovely visit, and I had learned a lot about how to pray. But the children were not miraculously healed as I had hoped and prayed for. Pastor Bill told me that sometimes God healed someone after a single prayer, but often he prayed numerous times before someone was fully healed. I found this both puzzling and encouraging. It was puzzling because I had always viewed healing prayer more or less like a light switch—it either worked or it didn't. It was encouraging because it helped me understand that healing could come in stages.

Pastor Bill pointed out how this was true when Jesus prayed for the blind man in Bethsaida:

They came to Bethsaida, and some people brought a blind man and begged Jesus to touch him. He took the blind man by the hand and led him outside the village. When he had spit on the man's eyes and put his hands on him, Jesus asked, "Do you see anything?"

He looked up and said, "I see people; they look like trees walking around."

Once more Jesus put his hands on the man's eyes. Then his eyes were opened, his sight was restored, and he saw everything clearly. (Mark 8:22–25)

I've read that passage many times, but it never truly gripped me until Pastor Bill prayed for Elizabeth. I went to Seattle with all the faith, hope, and love I had in me. A godly man prayed over her, and still we didn't get the healing we had hoped for. Remembering this story from Mark's Gospel helped me hold on to my faith, because it reminded me that healing is sometimes a journey rather than a light switch. This gave me hope for Elizabeth; it meant that our prayers for her weren't in vain simply because we didn't see an immediate result.

Like Robert Frost, Elizabeth's journey is on the road less traveled. Her "Mind" poem at the beginning of the chapter tells us about a deep, dark hole in her that is waiting for the light to seep within. She can't quite put it in words, and neither can I. Slowly, she is emerging.

Emergence

My senses are awakening
I feel brand-new.
I am on a road less traveled
But there are things I plan to do:
To speak to you.
I'll tell you all the things
You have wanted to know
I promise you the words will flow.

I am feeling new things as I get older. I am notic-
ing changes in my body and thoughts. I am feeling
stronger, and I need to speak.

We don't know why God has not yet healed Elizabeth completely.
We know that our prayers and God's healing power are an inter-
play between us and God. We are in a relationship that goes both
ways. The more persistent we are and the more we work together
with God, the more likely healing is to happen. Pastor Bill has
encouraged me to remember the parable of the persistent widow:

Then Jesus told them a parable about their need to pray always
and not to lose heart. He said, "In a certain city there was a
judge who neither feared God nor had respect for people. In
that city there was a widow who kept coming to him and saying,
'Grant me justice against my opponent.' For a while he refused;
but later he said to himself, 'Though I have no fear of God and
no respect for anyone, yet because this widow keeps bothering
me, I will grant her justice, so that she may not wear me out by

continually coming.'" And the Lord said, "Listen to what the unjust judge says. And will not God grant justice to his chosen ones who cry to him day and night? Will he delay long in helping them? I tell you, he will quickly grant justice to them. And yet, when the Son of Man comes, will he find faith on earth?" (Luke 18:1–8 NRSV)

With persistence and faith, we believe Elizabeth is being healed over time and will ultimately be fully healed. For some reason, her time has not yet come. If she is not completely healed before I die, you can be sure that "Why?" will be the first question I ask God.

What I haven't told you about Pastor Bill is that, with nineteen stents in his big heart, he has seen his share of suffering too. We joke that he's probably in the *Guinness World Records* book under "Most Stents." Pastor Bill doesn't fill his life with questions like "Why did God start all this stent business with that heart attack in my forties?" Instead he says, "I guess God wanted me to stop running that large Lutheran church and get about his business of quietly healing people." Pastor Bill is a How Person.

This journey in healing is also about healing my expectations of what Elizabeth should be. It is about acceptance. Elizabeth has taught me that at least right now and maybe forever, autism is part of who she is. Just as Temple Grandin's mother says in the movie *Temple Grandin*, autism makes a mind that is *different but not less*. The following dialogue also helps to put autism in perspective:

Elizabeth: **Is it good to have autism?**

Soma: There are good and bad about all situations. There are some good things about having autism. What do you think about it?

Elizabeth: **Don't want to talk about myself. Why is God so unclear about autism?**

Soma: Autism is an evolved state where the mental is highly evolved and there is no care for the body.

Elizabeth: **So, is it good?**

Soma: God is not wrong.

Elizabeth: **I am having trouble knowing myself.**

What is Elizabeth's prayer for healing?

Dear God

I need peace
And may my pain decrease.
I am not at ease
Can you help me please?
Make my pain cease
Dear God, I need peace.

I was worried that Elizabeth would think that God didn't love her because our prayers hadn't been answered. But Elizabeth's spirituality goes beyond her years. When we asked her about our visit with Pastor Bill she typed: **"I felt hope and peace."** She saw the healing we received: the hope and peace to carry on.

15

Joy

The Secret of How

Follow those who seek the truth and flee from those who've found it.

Václav Havel

Whale watching in Nova Scotia

Can't Give Up

Today is a new start
Not a man can stop me
I plan to make a change
To be the person that I should be
To prove that I am smart
It is real tough to be me
I hope that everyone realizes that
I am in here

(age 12)

I know I need to act like I am growing up, to make changes in my actions. I need to be good.

W hen I hurt myself, it helps."

There have been many dark moments in our journey, moments I've chosen not to make the focus of this book. Moments when the desperation is so great, it threatens to swallow me whole. Dark nights when fear and helplessness are my only companions. Days when hope feels dead and joy some distant memory.

It's then that I cry out, "Where are you, God? I'm here in the dark and I can't take much more of this."

"They make me think that I am of no use to myself or anyone. When I hurt myself, it helps."

Elizabeth's words haunt me in these dark times. To think that she would willingly substitute physical pain for emotional pain brings me to tears. She used to hit herself only once or twice a day, but now, with adolescence, the hitting has become more frequent and more aggressive. A multitude of doctors have not been able to find an answer. One of the many cruelties of autism is that it turns legions of otherwise capable people into help-less observers. We have been given a ringside seat to a torturous display of human suffering.

One recent afternoon, I got the bright idea to put Elizabeth's horseback riding helmet on her during a particularly violent out-burst. Elizabeth hit the helmet a couple of times, but she would not be defeated by it. She quickly turned to hitting herself in the mouth, where she could do maximal damage. Because she wears braces on

her teeth, her lips became a swollen, bloody mess before I realized the disaster I had created and grabbed the helmet off her head.

After *she* was back in control and settled down watching her videos again, I sobbed while dabbing her bloody lips. These are the darkest times, the times that stretch me to my breaking point. I have no greater sorrow in life than feeling helpless to relieve my children's suffering. How can we cling to joy in moments like this?

This isn't an idle question, for me or for any of us. In Dante's *Inferno*, above the gates of hell a sign reads, "Abandon all hope." I cannot think of a more apt description of hell—a place without hope. Yet the burden of autism can push us to live in that very place, even though it's more self-destructive than hitting ourselves in the head. Somehow, autism moms have to find a way to cling to hope with a tenacity that is stronger than autism's grip on our children. But how?

My answer: finding the joy in the smallest of moments. It is a conscious choice—a discipline, really—to seek and find these small flowers of joy in the crannied wall. When we lose our ability to experience joy, we lose our ability to hope. For me, hope is the handmaiden of joy.

To recognize joy is to know that there is a beauty greater than our pain, a goodness more powerful than our suffering. And just as with prayer, small joys lead to greater ones. When we learn to find the small joys sprouting through a barren landscape, we increase our ability to see even greater ones surrounding us on all sides.

But before we can find those joys, as Elizabeth has taught me, we must forgive. With mercy toward ourselves and others, we can release the anger that poisons the soul. Elizabeth recently told us:

> Today I am in a strange position in my life. I am
> forgiving everyone, one by one. I am also forgiving
> my anger. Anger possesses the self and blinds the
> mind. . . . I am forgiving my image in the mirror. . . .
> For the past two months I am making a list to forgive
> and it includes Mom and Dad too. I wish I never
> knew I was smart. That way I wouldn't have to real-
> ize my autism. I wish I did not have any education
> at all. I wish I had time to really forgive myself for
> being so hurtful. It is my speech.

Is Elizabeth's hurtfulness her speech, or is her lack of speech so hurtful to her? Both, I suspect, are true.

One of my guiding lights on this lifelong path of seeking for-giveness, truth, and joy in life is the late Henri Nouwen. When I am tempted to allow sorrow to rob me and my daughter of our joy, I hear Henri whispering that we always have the choice to live a moment as a cause of resentment or as a cause for joy.

Henri Nouwen, a Dutch-born priest who penned a treasure of books on the spiritual life, knew about these choices. At the height of his career, he left the comforts of the ivory tower to spend the last ten years of his life caring for the basic needs of the most vulnerable members of our society. It was in these years of humble service that Henri found the peace and joy that long eluded him in a life of spectacular professional achievements.

Henri's academic career included professorships at Notre Dame and Yale before he came to teach at Harvard (while I was a student there, ironically, but before I'd had any exposure to his remarkable writing). In the midst of a deep depression, he left Harvard to live at L'Arche Daybreak, a small community

in Toronto, Canada, for individuals with severe physical and mental challenges.

At L'Arche, Henri invested two hours each morning taking care of Adam Arnett, a man who could not speak or care for the most basic of his own needs. Henri lifted Adam out of bed and into his wheelchair, bathed him, brushed his teeth, combed his hair, and helped him raise a spoon to his mouth for his morning meal.

An author friend of Henri's visited him in his simple room one day and asked whether it would not be better for this accomplished man to use his precious time writing rather than in this manual labor. Henri responded that his friend did not understand: "I am not giving up anything. It is I, not Adam, who gets the main benefit from our friendship."

Henri understood that our most profound spiritual experiences are rarely found on the mountaintop. They are usually inextricably woven into the humblest acts of service for those in need. I must admit that at the end of a long day, I wish that Elizabeth could take her own shower. But while we strive to reach full independence, I will do my best to remember Henri serving Adam with joy and thanksgiving.

This is the nature of mercy, the nature of compassion: we enter into the life of another person in a deep and transformative way. Compassion means literally "to suffer with." Henri was no longer reading the beatitude "Blessed are the merciful, for they will be shown mercy" (Matt. 5:7). Instead, he was living it. In our simple acts of mercy and kindness, we live connected to each other and to our loving God.

Take Time to Pray

The power of prayer is soulfully strong
The Bible has told of it all along
Look to God, he will see you through
He wants to take care of you
Trust in him and believe

I need a lot of prayer. My life is hard. God, help me.

When Adam passed away unexpectedly at thirty-four, Henri had been preparing to write a theological discourse on the Apostles' Creed. Instead, he decided to simplify. He would write *Adam: God's Beloved*. In the introduction to *Adam*, Henri tells us that he has been searching his whole contemplative life for the way to live in the name of a loving God. With Adam's passing, Henri internalized the truth that each of us, no matter what our circumstances or station in life, is God's beloved.

For Henri, Adam became "my friend, my teacher, and my guide."[1] Likewise, through her perseverance and her poetry, Elizabeth has also become my teacher. She is teaching me to slow down, to appreciate the beauty in nature, and to be more patient. She is teaching me about love and the power of faith. She is teaching me to have compassion, because each of us is fighting a great battle.

I often call Elizabeth an "old soul" because she expresses to me a profound understanding of God and life that seems to go well beyond her years.

S omething inside of me

O ur inner strength

U nder skin and bone

L ifting us up from within

Living with Elizabeth and her autism has led me to ask many questions about life. How do we connect with those we love when there are no words? How do we balance acceptance of our children's differences with our desire to change them? How is God here with us in our suffering? How are we being healed? How do we balance life in the midst of such turmoil? How do we find joy and keep our hope alive?

I will spend the rest of my life seeking the answers to these questions.

Victor Frankl had his epiphany in Auschwitz: "For the first time in my life I saw the truth as it is set into song by so many poets, proclaimed as the final wisdom by so many thinkers. The truth—that love is the ultimate and the highest goal to which man can aspire. Then I grasped the meaning of the greatest secret that human poetry and human thought and belief have to impart: *The salvation of man is through love and in love.*"[2]

In *my* heart, even in the darkest moments, I know there is love in this world. And where there is love, joy and hope will follow.

Elizabeth said it better on one of our Christmas cards:

Joy is in the air.
Peace is everywhere.
Love is what we share.

Elizabeth's favorite poet, Emily Dickinson, writes about joy and hope. We try to read her poetry often because it is food for the soul. For me, Elizabeth embodies the spirit of Dickinson's bird in this poem:

> Hope is the thing with feathers
> That perches in the soul,
> And sings the tune without the words
> and never stops at all.[3]

Like Dickinson's bird, Elizabeth sings her own tune with persistence. No, not with persistence—she sings relentlessly.

Perhaps it's even simpler than that. From a young age, Elizabeth has replayed over and over again a particular scene from Disney's *Snow White and the Seven Dwarfs*. It is the scene where blackbirds fly out of a pie, startling Snow White. I used to think that it was just another of the meaningless, repetitive behaviors that can make us autism moms feel like we will go crazy. Now I know Elizabeth was telling me that she is one of those birds, trapped not in a pie but in her own silent cage. Long before we found a way in, she was begging to be set free.

Today Elizabeth takes great joy in birds and anything to do with flying. She loves to fly on airplanes, to fly kites, and to see raptors gliding overhead.

Over the Treetops

As wide as the sea
I noticed a seagull.
Did it see only the tree
Or did it see me?
I often wonder
How it would be
To fly over the treetops
And out to the sea.

I am very interested in anything that flies. It is amazing to me. Birds, airplanes, dragonflies, helicopters,
to name just a few. I love to go on an airplane and
be up in the clouds.

Elizabeth's love of flying brings to mind an Agnes Sanford
story that Pastor Bill likes to tell. He was having lunch with Agnes
and told her about the thrill he had riding in a glider. Despite
being in her mid-eighties, Agnes was enthusiastic to experience
it. Unfortunately, when the day of the flight arrived, Agnes was
not feeling well and had to call the pilot to cancel the trip. After
she hung up the phone, she told Edith, the woman who helped
take care of her in her later years, "I am going to go lie down
and take a glider ride of my own."

An hour later, Edith looked in on Agnes, and she was lying
on her bed completely at peace. She was taking her glider ride
back home.

We are here on earth for a brief stay, and then we are called home.

In "Arriving Home" from *The Dance of Life: Weaving Sorrows and Blessings into One Joyful Step*, Henri Nouwen shows us his "How" side when he writes:

> The question is not "How am I to find God?" but "How am I to let myself be found by him?". . . The question is not "How am I to love God?" but "How am I to let myself be loved by God?" . . . God is the father who watches and waits for his children, runs to meet them, embraces them, pleads with them, begs and urges them to come home.[4]

Henri loved this vision of the prodigal son, which was so movingly painted by Rembrandt. I understand this painting now in ways that I could not have when I was younger. The painting captures the relentless, yearning love of God—the fierce love parents have for their children. Just as we fight to free our children from autism's grip and draw them more fully into the life for which they were created, so too does God struggle to free us from the grip of our sorrow, our worry, and our self-centeredness and into the life of love for which we were made.

You can see the marks of this struggle on the father's face in Rembrandt's painting. It's a combination of love, joy, and sorrow, all bound up in his compassionate embrace of the son who had finally returned home. The father and son fit together like two pieces of a puzzle.

One of Rembrandt's greatest gifts was his ability to capture the imprint of our lives on our faces as we age. Our loves, our hopes, our fears, and our sorrows—all of them are eventually written on our faces. In the same way that a river cuts through

a canyon, carving out a riverbed that sets the river's course, our shared lives cut grooves in each other. Our shared joys and sorrows connect us. It's a painful process, but it's also one of great beauty.

The struggles I've shared with Elizabeth have carved deep grooves into our souls. We are bound together in ways that are unique to us. I believe the same is true with God. My life has been a journey of inching toward and slipping away from God. Back and forth, back and forth. There is a groove carved in my heart that only God can fill. I'd like to think I've worn a groove into God's heart as well. And one day I will go home, where our grooves fit perfectly together, and I will rest in God's embrace.

On this earth, my joy with Elizabeth comes in those quiet times when we are walking in the woods or sitting on the couch together reading a book. These are the times when she lets me into her world. These are the times when we could not be closer, when we fit together like pieces of a puzzle. I hold her in my arms, and she knows that I believe in her and I will be there for her.

Art is another shining example of shared joy. We started out small and have gradually moved to bigger venues. Our first adventures were exhibits of local artists in the library. Next we went to a small museum, always allowing Elizabeth to set the pace, which meant we were kind of jogging through the rooms. Now we plan trips to cities that have great museums, and the pace has slowed. It's still faster than I prefer, but we take our adventures in art as a victory. We just completed a series of college lectures on great paintings, and Elizabeth told us she loves Vincent van Gogh. Many reproductions of his paintings now hang in her room.

Van Gogh happens to be my favorite artist, and with Henri Nouwen's help, I have come to understand why. Henri taught a seminar at Yale Divinity School in the 1970s called "The Ministry of Vincent van Gogh." In the foreword to the book *Van Gogh and*

God, Henri fondly remembers that course and "how we would spend long hours together in silence, simply gazing at the slides of Vincent's work. I did not try to explain much or analyze much. I simply wanted the students to have a direct experience of the ecstasy and agony of this painter who shared his desperate search for meaning."[5] This is definitely a course I should have taken.

Henri believed that Van Gogh's universal appeal is rooted in his art's tender reflection of life as a pilgrimage. Van Gogh had been an evangelistic preacher before finding his ministry in art. In November 1876, a young Van Gogh mounted the pulpit of a small Methodist church in Richmond, England, to give his first sermon:

> We are pilgrims on the earth and strangers—we have come from afar and we are going far—the journey of our life goes from the loving breast of our Mother on earth to the arms of our Father in heaven. Everything on earth changes—we have no abiding city here—it is the experience of everyone.[6]

Throughout his life, Van Gogh melded the philosophies of East and West. He was fascinated by and collected Japanese "floating world" prints that mirror the Buddhist notion that life is in constant flux.

My reasons for loving Van Gogh's art are rooted in his use of color and texture. Simply put, the vibrant colors bring me joy, and something about the thickness of the paint makes each work dance with energy and life. You need to see a Van Gogh painting in person to appreciate the dynamism of those great dollops of paint. The same can be said for Elizabeth: you need to see her in person, to be present with her, to feel the energy and life that is within her.

Maybe I love Van Gogh even more because he may have had autism. We will never know for sure, but there are many "special" people who have made great contributions to the world due to

their obsessive, creative, and perhaps "autistic" minds: Albert Einstein, Lewis Carroll, and Sir Isaac Newton to name a few.

Philosopher and theologian Paul Tillich linked painting with poetry: "All arts create symbols for a level of reality which cannot be reached in any other way. A picture and a poem reveal elements of reality which cannot be approached scientifically. In the creative work of art we encounter reality in a dimension which is closed for us without such works."[7]

The ability for art to communicate beyond words—not just without them but beyond them—brings me back to Elizabeth. We all share Elizabeth's struggle to communicate. All of us have tried to find words for our deepest thoughts and feelings about who we are. We easily speak the most meaningless, mundane things, but the most important things to us, the dearest things, are the hardest to find words for. This is the goal of the artist, and for me, Elizabeth's art—her poetry—communicates more than words that she would speak.

There are times when Elizabeth does speak to me. We laugh and dance together. This is my vision for her, fully healed. She is the same beautiful child she is now, but without the fetters of autism. She doesn't strike herself in frustration. She is happy and healthy. I believe this vision will come to pass because I persist in the hope that the Love that binds us together will heal her, body and soul. We know that there are three things that endure—faith, hope, and love—and the greatest of these is love.

Today, a decade after her initial diagnosis, our battle continues. Despite all of her challenges, Elizabeth embraces life and knows that she is being healed every day. And miracle of miracles, she is starting to communicate with her voice. Sometimes while driving down the road, I will hear "pizza" behind me when she sees a sign for her favorite food. Because I am thrilled to hear

her voice, we pull over and stop for a slice. "Fire" is another favorite word, which she says when we light birthday candles or burn wood in the fireplace.

Fire

By the fireside
All aglow
All the colors
How they flow
Red to orange
Yellow to blue.
That only names a few.
Just like the feelings
A warm fire brings.
It makes your heart
Want to sing.

Looking into a fire is fascinating to me. It is comforting on a winter night when there is snow on the ground. The fire seems alive the way it moves and changes color.

In this second coming of her language, the few words that she struggles to get out are not always clear, but they are evidence of her valiant efforts to overcome the shackles of her autism. For me, her voice is a joyful noise, and I cheer her every word.

As Elizabeth writes, she has a "Bright Future." This poem was introduced as the first of this book and appears again here

in hopes that you read it differently now. In the first chapter, it showed her optimism; now it is a call to action. With the right encouragement and support, our children are strong and able. The beauty of nature found in the tall tree, shining sun, and glimmering lake are reflected in them. Elizabeth wants us to see every child and praise God for a glorious creation.

Bright Future

When you see
A tree
Think of me
Growing strong and tall.

When you see
The sun shining brightly
Think of me
Tough and mighty.

When you see
The water on the lake
Think of the future
I plan to make.

Me
Strong
Mighty
Free

The How People in this book have given me the strength to tell you Elizabeth's story. By now, you have probably guessed my secret: I've never met many of these How People. They are

the authors who have touched my heart and imprinted on my soul the knowledge that *I am not alone*. The How People I have met both in person and in print are with us on our journey. The hope and joy in their stories inspire us to fight our battle another day.

Epilogue

All the darkness in the world can't extinguish the light from a single candle.

St. Francis of Assisi

As this book goes to print, I want to share a few updates with you.

First, there is some amazing news about Cheryl, my roof badminton friend, who has been in constant pain for more than two years. She tells the story better than I can in this email:

Dear prayer warriors,

God has been moving mountains in my life. I was told by a specialist that what I have is incurable. I told him we were praying and that God knew better. God has led me to a physical therapist in Nevada and he believes I am a good candidate to be cured. Please join me in praying that God gives the therapist the

insight to know what is wrong with me and the ability to fix it.
Thank you for all your prayers. God knows mountains could
not be moved without them.
   Love, Cheryl

Despite the difficulties of travel for someone who cannot sit without severe pain, Cheryl flew to Nevada and had three days of treatment with the physical therapist. She is now healed.

Cheryl's steadfast faithfulness has been a rock for me during our own crisis these past eighteen months. Elizabeth has not been well. Almost every day, all day, someone has to sit beside her to deflect her fists or knees from hitting her face. She sleeps little at night and often needs me to be with her as she struggles mightily to find the brief moments of rest that sleep affords her.

In spite of her previous success in the mainstream classroom, Elizabeth has needed Terri and me to teach her at home this academic year. For six hours each day, we do ten minutes of an academic subject and then take a five minute break. Because Elizabeth has a photographic memory, she is ahead in all of her classes, and we supplement her studies with college lectures on art and philosophy.

During this time, we traveled to countless specialists, many of whom simply attributed these behaviors to her autism. But I have come to know autism over the past thirteen years, and of course I have come to know Elizabeth as well. This self-injurious behavior is not the autism, nor the Elizabeth that I know. Something else is going on. But, once again, it takes time for the medical science to catch up with our lived experiences of illness. The science just isn't there yet to guide us.

Elizabeth described how it felt for her to endure this suffering during one of her home lessons when she typed, "**Bugs are eating my brains.**"

She had never used this type of disturbing language to describe her pain before, so I was beside myself with worry. At this point, the facial blows were coming every forty seconds, and I was convinced more than ever that something was ravaging her brain. After reading everything I could find on self-injurious behaviors, I asked several doctors if a virus might be the cause. They responded that there was scant support in the medical research literature. Brain viruses are rare.

So the doctors looked elsewhere. Elizabeth had sedated MRI scans and a forty-eight-hour in-hospital EEG, but they found no tumors or evidence of seizures. Finally, I convinced one of our doctors to do a special virus test which would take months to process. With Elizabeth in such agony, how could I not continue searching for the cause as rare as a virus might be?

This was a dark time of trying medication after medication. We just tried to get through each day. Nothing helped very much or for very long. Some medications made her much worse and were immediately discontinued. Every time I placed a new pill in her mouth, I felt terrible because I believed that we were not dealing with the root cause, only its terrible outward effect. Many nights I cried myself to sleep and asked God how I could publish a book about hope when I felt so hopeless.

After one particularly bad meltdown, Elizabeth gave me the equivalent of my dad's "Buck up!" when she typed, "**Get me professional help.**" She was right. Besides focusing on her brain chemistry, we needed help managing the uncontrollable behaviors.

Soon after, we headed to the Kennedy Krieger Institute, part of Johns Hopkins Hospital, for two weeks of intensive, outpatient behavioral treatment. "Intensive" means five hours a day, five days a week in an eight-by-eight-foot padded, windowless, blue room with Elizabeth, three therapists, Terri, and me. Acknowledging Elizabeth's intelligence and seeking her input in the process, the therapists tailored a Cognitive Behavioral Therapy program to help her work through her anger.

The therapists treated Elizabeth as a teammate, not as a silent conscript. They read her poetry and had conversations with her to better understand what made her angry. Not surprisingly, **"treating me like a baby"** and **"taking away my computer"** were at the top of the list. In subtle ways, they acknowledged she was "in there," and that respect made all the difference to both of us.

During one of our sessions, Elizabeth told us, **"Mickey makes me hit myself."** I was shocked. We were surrounded by Disney items in that blue padded room because we thought that her usual stable of books and movies would be a comfort to her. But they had become an obsession. The therapists suggested that we think of it as a drug addiction and wean her off of them slowly. Months later, we asked Elizabeth how it felt to be Disney-free, and she typed, **"My head is clear."**

While our time at Kennedy Krieger did not eliminate the problem behaviors, it gave us techniques to diffuse many situations and deflect the blows if they came. On our last day, Elizabeth typed, **"These people do good work."**

When we finally got the virus results, I read them with mixed emotions: Elizabeth tested positive. While I am relieved to have a path to pursue, I am afraid to think about the treatment needed for a cure. Once again we are reluctant pioneers in medical science, heading out on yet another journey we didn't sign

up for. Her poetry captures the hopes and fears during these days, weeks, and months of physical, emotional, and spiritual tumult.

Reflections

It made my heart bleed
As I felt freed
Destined to stay in pain
But finding myself flying again
What a coincidence

I felt I was drowning in anger. I was feeling hopeless. The anger would not go away.

When I have been at my lowest, God has seen my tears and repeatedly prompted special friends to let me know I haven't been forgotten. These How People have gotten me through: my mother, Sean, Jane, Charlie, Jim, Judy, Fred, Laurie, Cheryl, and so many others who have given me words of encouragement when I sorely needed them.

It was Cheryl who called me one sad Tuesday night when I usually had my prayer time with Pastor Bill. Her loving words poured over me: "I know that I'm not Pastor Bill, but I wanted to make sure that you were not alone tonight." You see, this was the first Tuesday that Bill wasn't calling me. I was scheduled to be with him that week in Seattle on his eightieth birthday, but his health took a turn for the worse, and his family asked me to postpone my trip. He so yearned to be one with God. Now he finally is.

On one of our last Tuesday calls, Bill told me he was sure that Elizabeth *would* be healed. He could see her well and speaking to us. I remembered this beautiful vision when her virus test results came in. They weren't expected for another month but arrived on the day Bill was laid to rest. I took it as a sign that God hadn't forgotten us.

A few weeks after getting those results, we started a new natural medication that activates the body's immune system to fight viruses. We are early in this treatment, and our history in the autism battle tells us that there are likely to be both triumphs and setbacks ahead of us. But at this moment, after only seven weeks of treatment, Elizabeth is free from the horror of constantly hitting herself. I believe that we are now on the right path for Elizabeth to be fully healed and, finally, to speak. Her recent poems tell me she believes it too.

Cure for Winter

I feel His presence all around
In the flowers blooming and the birds returning
The Earth is ready to begin anew
And I am too

My journey with Elizabeth has been one of mind, body, and spirit. Recently she told me she believes she can read my mind. After my initial surprise, I recalled many times when her typing reflected just what I was thinking, even though I was across the room. I wish that I could be in her mind and body for just one moment to see and feel the world as she sees and feels it. As close as we are spiritually, she remains a mystery to me in many ways.

Alfred, Lord Tennyson wrote about the beauty of this mystery in his poetry:

> Flower in the crannied wall,
> I pluck you out of the crannies,
> I hold you here, root and all, in my hand,
> Little flower—but if I could understand
> What you are, root and all, and all and all,
> I should know what God and man is.[1]

This poem has been special to me since my graduation from high school. On that day, I was supposed to give the valedictorian address, and my text was to be a reflection on "Flower in the Crannied Wall" and its notion that although God and our fellow human beings would largely remain a mystery to us, we could nonetheless gain some important insights into that mystery from loving all of God's creation, even the smallest and most overlooked elements.

I never did get to give that speech because I refused to submit it for censorship. Maybe that public muzzling has helped me empathize with Elizabeth a bit more. If nothing else, it shows that Elizabeth and I share the stubborn gene. While the whole affair hurt me deeply at the time, I now see the benefit: it burned that poem into my heart, which has changed the way I see the world.

Elizabeth is my little flower, relentlessly breaking through autism with her poetry. Like the flowers in the sidewalk cracks and crannied walls, she is a quiet miracle. I may never understand her fully, just as I will never fully understand God, but our journey together will continue to be filled with love and awe until it reaches its ultimate, glorious destination. To use the words of Saint Paul, "All that I know now is partial and incomplete, but

then I will know everything completely, just as God now knows me completely" (1 Cor. 13:12 NLT).

Alice in Wonderland sang, "You can learn a lot of things from the flowers." I know I have. My little flower has taught me to look beyond the cracks in my life and see the beauty in all of God's creation. It's a lesson we can all learn.

Look down for a minute. Do you see only a cracked sidewalk? Look closer. God has left you a love note.

"How People" Gallery

Corrie, Tim, Annie, Jen, and Cathy

Elizabeth and Soma

Jim and Elizabeth

Judy and Alex

Al and Junior

Sean

Terri and Elizabeth

Kathy and
her kids

Jane and her miracle babies

Cheryl and Virginia

Elizabeth
and Mimi

Elizabeth and Pastor Bill

Fred

Elizabeth and Kerri

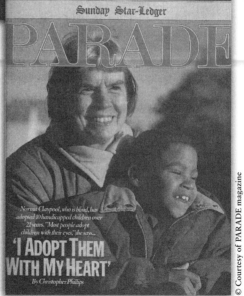

Norma Claypool

Charlie

Tammy and Charles

Nan and Pop

Acknowledgments

I am not a writer by training or disposition, but I promised Elizabeth I would do anything in my power to get her poetry and message of hope out into the world. Many loving people rallied around us, and we are grateful for their time and talents in making this book a reality.

In particular, three angels went above and beyond, reading countless drafts and improving them immeasurably.

I wrote about Sean in the chapter "Healing." Who would have thought that passing notes in English class would lead to this? Your energy, enthusiasm, and writing craftsmanship added structure, depth, and beauty to this book.

I introduced Charlie in "Suffering." Who would have thought that a chance meeting in Tibet would produce this? Your production skills and talented team gave us a television show that created the platform for telling this story.

I wrote about Jim in "Wall Street and Autism." Who would have thought that out of the ashes of LockStar would come this? Your encouragement to tell our story and relentless belief in Elizabeth helped us find our voices.

Thank you, Pastor Bill, Cheryl, and Sean (yes, you get double billing), for lifting this project up in prayer and sending me words of encouragement in emails and text messages.

Thank you, Soma, for giving Elizabeth an escape from her silent cage.

Thank you, Terri, for being there for Elizabeth every day for more than a decade.

Thank you, Fred and Jane, for your friendships, close readings, and encouragement to tell Elizabeth's story.

Thank you, Drs. Sid, Jeff, and Charles, for guiding us through all of the biomedical interventions.

Thank you, Dr. Dosia, for taking a special interest in Elizabeth and helping her get well.

Thank you to all who worked so hard and lovingly on our home-based educational team: Terri, Tina, Becky, Susan, Corey, Michelle, Chris, Debbie, Kara, Missy, Joann, Pat, and the many others whose names are now lost to me.

Thank you, teachers and administrators at Elizabeth's school, for opening your minds and hearts to educate and embrace a special child.

Thank you, Richard, for introducing me to your thoughtful agent, Kathy.

Thank you, Jennifer and Wendy, for improving this book with your keen editorial eyes.

Thank you, Revell team, for your commitment to getting Elizabeth's message of hope out to the world.

Thank you, Ray, for staying the course for the children.

Thank you, Mom, for being my mother, in every beautiful sense of the word.

Thank you, Gale, Charles, and Elizabeth, for the love, joy, and wonder you have brought into my life.

Notes

Chapter 2 Autism

1. Thomas Wolfe, *Look Homeward, Angel* (New York: Charles Scribner's Sons, 1929), 1.

Chapter 7 Community

1. William Wordsworth, "Ode: Imitations of Immortality from Recollections of Early Childhood," in Sir Arthur Thomas Quiller-Couch, ed., *The Oxford Book of English Verse* (Oxford: Clarendon, 1919); online at Bartleby.com, www.bartleby .com/101/.

2. Malcolm Gladwell, *The Tipping Point* (New York: Little, Brown and Company, 2000), 38.

Chapter 8 Nature

1. Helen Keller, *The World I Live In* (London: Hodder & Stoughton, 1904), 119; available online at Project Gutenberg, http://www.gutenberg.org/files/27683 /27683-h/27683-h.htm.

2. Ralph Waldo Emerson, *Nature* (Boston: James Munroe and Company, 1849); available online at Project Gutenberg, http://www.gutenberg.org/files/29433 /29433-h/29433-h.htm.

Chapter 9 Hopes and Dreams

1. *Temple Grandin*, directed by Mick Jackson (New York: HBO Home Video, 2010), DVD.

2. Christopher Phillips, "I Adopted Them with My Heart," *Parade*, December 25, 1988, 4–5.

3. Eustacia Cutler, *A Thorn in My Pocket* (Arlington, TX: Future Horizons, 2004), 161.

4. Jenny McCarthy, *Louder Than Words: A Mother's Journey in Healing Autism* (New York: Dutton, 2007), 189, emphasis in original.

5. Bari Weiss, "Life Among the 'Yakkity Yaks,'" The Weekend Interview, *Wall Street Journal*, February 23, 2010, http://online.wsj.com/article/SB100014240527 4870352570457506112356400751 4.html. Grandin's term "Aspberger" is a form of high-functioning autism more commonly spelled "Asperger's."

6. Victor Frankl, *Man's Search for Meaning* (Boston: Beacon Press, 1959), 65–66.

Chapter 11 Families

1. "The Garden/All in the Golden Afternoon, *Walt Disney's Alice in Wonderland* (1951; Burbank, CA: Walt Disney Home Video, 2004), DVD.

Chapter 12 Suffering

1. As quoted in "Science: Death of a Genuis," *Time*, May 2, 1955, http://www .time.com/time/magazine/article/0,9171,866292,00.html.

2. M. Scott Peck, *The Road Less Traveled: A New Psychology of Love, Traditional Values and Spiritual Growth*, 25th ann. ed. (New York: Touchstone, 2003), 15.

3. Rabbi Harold Kushner, *When Bad Things Happen to Good People* (New York: Avon Books, 1983), 4.

Chapter 13 God

1. Luke Timothy Johnson, *Living Jesus: Learning the Heart of the Gospel* (New York: HarperOne, 1999), 60.

2. William Stillman, *Autism and the God Connection* (Naperville, IL: Source-Books, 2006), 184–98.

3. Richard Foster, *Celebration of Discipline: The Path to Spiritual Growth* (New York: HarperCollins, 1978), 100–101.

4. Eberhard Arnold, "Why We Choose Silence Over Dialogue," *The Plough*, a publication of the Bruderhof communities, no. 11 (July/August 1985): 12; as quoted in Foster, *Celebration of Discipline*, 165.

Chapter 15 Joy

1. Henri Nouwen, *Adam: God's Beloved* (Maryknoll, NY: Orbis Books, 1997), 15.

2. Frankl, *Man's Search for Meaning*, 37.

3. Emily Dickinson, *The Complete Poems of Emily Dickinson* (Boston: Little, Brown, 1924); Bartleby.com, 2000, www.bartleby.com/113/.

4. Henri J. M. Nouwen, *The Dance of Life: Weaving Sorrows and Blessings into One Joyful Step*, ed. Michael Ford (Notre Dame, IN: Ave Maria Press, 2005), 206–7.

5. Cliff Edwards, *Van Gogh and God* (Chicago: Loyola Press, 1989), ix–x.

6. Ibid., 1.

7. Paul Tillich, *The Essential Tillich: An Anthology of the Writings of Paul Tillich*, ed. F. Forrester Church (Chicago: University of Chicago Press, 1999), 42.

Epilogue

1. Alfred, Lord Tennyson, "Flower in the Crannied Wall," *A Collection of Poems* (Garden City, NY: Doubleday, 1972), 318.

Elizabeth M. Bonker is a thirteen-year-old young lady with autism who cannot yet speak but who writes deeply revealing poetry, which was featured on PBS's *Religion & Ethics Newsweekly*. She excels in mainstream public school with an educational aide.

Virginia G. Breen is the mother of three beautiful children, two of whom are profoundly affected by autism. Besides working to heal her children, Virginia is a venture capitalist investing in high-tech companies, and she sits on both corporate and nonprofit boards. Previously, she studied computer science at Harvard, business at Columbia, and philosophy in Singapore. She now studies relentlessly at the school of autism.

Elizabeth and Virginia live in northern New Jersey.

Visit
www.IAmInHereBook.com
for additional resources
and information.

Features include information on
educational, behavioral, and medical
interventions as well as book and internet
resources for further reading.